Thank you to my husband.

You held me while I dislodged every bullet, and you've loved me all the way back to myself.

Thank you to my friends and family, by blood and by choice.

You caught me every time I jumped, and you lit candles every time I was lost in the dark.

To our sweet pup Dilly who never left my side, and whose sleepy snores made me smile through the worst chapters.

And to every sensitive soul out there, continuing to fight for what is in your heart, ripping yourself open to heal every wound. Thank God for you.

Should you ever be buried under an avalanche, you're supposed to spit and see which direction it falls so you know which way to start digging out.

S'good to know.

I wish it was that simple to find your way out of psychological abuse, but usually it makes things worse if you spit on people.

Too Sensitive

By Rebecca Garifo Ph.D.

Printed in the United States of America

First Printing, 2018

Names and locations in this book have been
changed to respect privacy.

*S*o, let's just pretend for a minute, that I'm *not* crazy.

What if, for the sake of hypothesis, all the nightmares, sleepless nights and anxiety ridden days, multiplying physical ailments, ongoing spiritual conversations and synchronicities, and a lifetime of nagging suspicions, *aren't* just my own wild childish imagination? What if it's all real, it's all been in the background of my mind for all these years, nibbling away at the foundation of my oblivion?

What if I'm *not* just, too sensitive?

I've been asking myself this question for thirty years. I've been called crazy all my life, "…crazy just like your mother," so *that* I'm accustomed to. But this idea of trusting my own knowing, believing my own memories? *That's* new. That feels dangerous. I'm addicted to self-analysis, teetering on self-flogging. I wanna fix things, I wanna get to the bottom of things and understand where we didn't see eye to eye, even if it means I'm the one that's completely off their rocker, I never stop wanting resolve. In all the letters I've written, or the hours crying and pleading for confirmation, I never stopped to think, "What if it's not all *me*?" What if I could never find the resolution or keep the peace because I'm not the one causing the problems? What if I'm not as awful and insane as they say I am?

But that's just crazy though, right?

I'm gonna be real honest with you, I still question my sanity on the daily. I feel like I'm swimming at the deep end of the pool for the first time without my water wings. But here I am. Paddling along, doin' just fine despite the prophecies of my demise and inevitable horrific failure that came from my own fear, and the mouths of many people I love.

Sometimes when we've been hitting a wall for years, we have to go backwards, we have to retrace our steps until we see a new path appear. People will see us throw it in reverse and say we're regressing, we're making a huge mistake, "that's just too bad…" they'll say. But what if we're actually *finally* finding our way outta the maze?

We're brave enough to try another way instead of just cursing our misfortune, blaming the brick and mortar in front of us for the lives we're damned to. We realize the walls we've been knocking our heads against in desperation, may actually be there to clearly say, "This isn't the way baby." Maybe we've been trying to change people all along, and finally realized, *that's* not it, that's not what we're here to do. We become sick, we experience loss and failure. We get divinely redirected by what often appears as catastrophic circumstances.

We finally turn to face ourselves.

This book is to share my steps I've retraced, and the doors I've avoided opening for a long time. Parts of myself I wanted to get as far away from as possible, as quickly as possible, missing the signs along the way as I ran faster and faster.

I hesitated in writing the details of many conversations and misunderstandings, sometimes it's more comforting to just chalk it up to me being dramatic again. Things may sound petty and childish, and I don't really *enjoy* coming off as whiney or pointing fingers, but to tell the whole truth, I must include my stubborn and fiery nature.

The more distance I've put between myself and these stories, the more the pieces have come together, and when it comes to the insidious core of gaslighting and emotional abuse, welp, the devil's *in* the details.

It's in the silent looks, the quick sharp remarks, the omissions no one else sees. The absolute void of empathy or remorse when our hearts have been shattered and we're crying for the thousandth time. This is where we lose our hope, our grip on reality, our belief we'll *ever* know truth. Our spirits slowly seep out of the holes punched through our skin every day, we don't understand why our lights continue to dim no matter how hard we stoke the fire. We're in a race against time to solve our own murder mystery before it's too late. I'm sharing this in hopes that it helps you put some pieces together and patch some holes in your own heart.

Now, I'm gonna go ahead and warn you, I tend to go in circles and ya *might* feel a lil disoriented before you get halfway through this book, but bear with me. We'll make it out together I promise. That feeling of being caught in the undertow, being put through the washing machine and not knowing which way is up or how the pieces fit, well, that's just what psychological abuse feels like. I promise you, it'll make sense in the end. So whether you're lost in my stories or swimming the circles in your own healing, keep going, you're gonna make it out. I promise you that.

There is so much to love in this world, and so many to share it with. What we can understand, we can heal. For what we can feel compassion, we can forgive, and even with time, love.

x

CHAPTER ONE

"You are the shatterer of darkness.
Wherever joyous laughter rings, darkness
cannot reside. Do not run and hide. SHINE."

Channeled in 2011

I was finishing up my breakfast on the porch of
our studio apartment. Joe and I had moved there a few
months before to make a new start for ourselves and our
relationship, give us some space to breathe again. The
last year had been rough on both of us. My bare feet
slapped against the pooling water as I showered my
potted Impatients. Their soft violet faces were thriving
and reaching for the morning sun as it bent around the
corners of our building.

It was still early yet, I've always liked to have a couple hours of quiet to journal and talk to my spiritual guardians before I have to get ready for work, but this morning, I'd already been feeling a sense of urgency since I'd opened my eyes. It had only been forty-eight hours since I'd kissed my mom's cheek and hugged her trembling shoulders. My bottom lip was shaking as I left her holding her shower essentials and booties at the hospital. I'd prayed and prayed the doctors and nurses could help her fight her demons better than I'd been able to.

I just wanted her to feel love, to feel peace, to finally forgive herself. This woman who'd taught me the essentials of dancing to *Earth Wind and Fire*, *The Doobie Brothers*, and *Chicago*. That watching *Funny Girl* and eating brownies could cure the blues. She wanted to go to concerts, see plays, and attend every powwow that came near us, always keeping framed pictures of Native women and children on her walls. I slept with rabbit skins on my pillows and my prized rock collections of fool's gold and amethysts. My sister and I would wake up on St. Patty's day to green food coloring in our gallon of milk and toilet bowls. After making chocolate chip cookies, she'd always hand me the spatula as if it were a fairy's wand. She could make the smallest things magical.

There were mornings I'd come into her bedroom and she'd be curled on her side, her back to the door, squeezing her pillow to her chest like a child holding onto their teddy. She'd been laying there for hours just listening to the radio. Her eyes always told me she just couldn't do it today. Her Wayne Dyer cassette tape sat on her night stand next to her alarm clock radio. I remember the rainbow across its plastic cover, and even as a child, I knew she was looking for something, desperately.

The urgency I'd been avoiding all morning had come with a message, "Call your mom. Call your mom. Call your mom." The ward she was in had two separate land lines with two cordless phones which were circulated between patients, so it was a roll of the dice callin' the place, ya never knew exactly who was gonna be answering on the other end.

"Ha-loooOOoow!?"

"Hi! Yeah um, good morning! I'm looking for my mom, Beverly Ma-"

"Oh yes! She's on the other cordless phone right now, hold on!"

My stomach dropped. Seven in the morning was a little early for her to already be making phone calls.

"Yeah here she is hold on!"

"Oh ok, thank you!"

"Rebecca?"

"Mom? What's goin' on?"

"Hold on, I'm on the other phone with your sister- Yeah, Samantha? I'll call you later ok, Rebecca just called on the other phone. Uh huh…uh huh…I love you… ok, buh bye. Hey my Be."

"Hey mom, so what's…what's goin' on?"

"Oh Rebecca… I don't even wanna tell you."

"I mean, obviously it's somethin'. I've had a feelin' I should call you all mornin' 'n you were already on the phone with Sam."

"Your mommy's just…not alright Rebecca. I've got to tell you. …I've been wantin' to hurt somebody…I've been thinkin' about it for a while now."

I swallowed the lump in my throat and shut my eyes tight, forcing myself to listen to what she was saying.

"Who are you wantin' to hurt mom?"

"Ronda, across the street."

I'd heard her talk obsessively about Ronda for the last year. Ronda's convertible, Ronda's boyfriend, Ronda's grandkids.

"Mom…" I sighed, "Why do you wanna hurt Miss Ronda?"

"Rebecca, she's everything I'm not."

"Oh man…"

I shut my eyes again and rubbed the soft flower petals, so fragile between my fingerstips. They'd not only survived but continued to blossom and grow stronger when I'd forgotten to water them for days at a time in the strong summer heat. Their colors had remained bright regardless.

"It's gonna be ok Rebecca… it's gonna be ok." I assured myself.

She waited on the other end for what I was gonna say. She's always been good at dropping bombs and then hanging around to see if I emerge from the rubble this time.

I kept my eyes closed, breathing in and out, rubbing that petal between my fingers, like I'd done as a kid with the floppy ear on my favorite stuffed animal. I'd wanted a lamb, and gotten a rabbit instead, but that didn't stop me from calling her Lamb Chop. Eventually I forgot she wasn't even a lamb in the first place. I have

15

a way of doing that with things in my life. If it's not what I wanna see, I'll just shut my eyes. I'll name it something else altogether. I'll hold to my chest the very thing that I know is a lie. I'll pull the covers around me and defiantly squeeze it tighter.

The vision I'd been having for months came flashing into my mind like a recalled memory, haunting me with what I didn't wanna see. Over and over, I'd seen myself walking into her home, screaming for her and rounding the corner to the kitchen to see her standing there, covered in blood that wasn't her own. "Mom what have you done." I say. She just stares at me, blank, not a word. Then I see blue lights pulling up outside her kitchen window.

No matter how tight we shut our eyes sometimes, the truth still finds its way into our vision. The light bends around our corners, begging us to keep growing, to receive life. It has a way of silencing our screams, no matter how loud our defiance. It transforms our rage into a still, soft, unshakable knowing.

For me, the truth has come up in pieces throughout my life, like paint chipping off of an old house after a hard rain. Storms have a way of doing that, unveiling our bare beams and exposing our structural damage. I realize there are parts of me that

16

were never truly me at all, only what someone's painted over me.

I was around six years old, and my mom rummaged through her purse as we sat in the old Buick outside Revco. A middle aged man was making cute faces and smiling at a puppy tucked under his arm, looking both ways before crossing the parking lot.

"What a cute little dog," my mother said, pausing her excavation to squint at the windshield, "He probably uses it to attract small children." She lowered her gaze and raised an eyebrow at me. "Trust no one." her eyes snarled.

I just remember thinking, "Oh my, gosh. *That's* how you see the world!?"

We haven't always had the same outlook on life, my mother 'n I. I think that's probably true for a lot of us. She always self-diagnosed herself, always telling everyone she had, "The Pollyanna Complex" but I never really saw her as having a truly positive outlook at all. Not when I could hear her teeth grinding the harder she smiled, and her fingers turn to fists the more agreeable she became.

I understand where she was coming from though, very well.

I understand wanting to feel positive and happy and kind, *so badly,* that you'll choke anyone to death who dare try to stop you. Smiling so fucking hard our cheeks ache. Namaste-ing and Love & Light-ing ourselves to fucking death. Painting inspirational quotes over our wounds and praying it doesn't rain.

That shit's-

Fucking.

Exhausting.

And even though there were times it felt like my mother would sooner use my dying breath to blow up her birthday balloons, she's taught me the importance of speaking your truth. The catastrophic destruction of avoiding it. And the miraculous healing in trusting it.

She taught me to trust that sneaking suspicion of foul play when someone's spouting inspirational quotes and preaching their overwhelming humility a little too loud.

To learn and navigate the line between trauma-induced paranoia, and divine street-smart wisdom.

To understand that truth brings freedom, and freedom unveils our joy, but that don't mean the process won't hurt like a *bitch*. Sometimes a real major bitch.

My mom has stretched my heart to reach capacities I never thought possible, like no one else ever could.

CHAPTER TWO

"Somebody tell me why I work so hard
for you."
Everything She Wants
Wham!

*W*e went to court when I was five to have our
Grandpa Charles tried and sentenced for sexual abuse.
Our mom had already obsessively read *Good Touch*
Bad Touch to my older sister and I before anything was
ever said. That was until my sister Samantha, had a
breakdown before our regular visit to his and Grandma
Fran's home in Tennessee.

I can smell the cold concrete and oil drips in the
garage leading into their house, and the maroon Subaru.
Fran's white octagonal china with fresh poured coffee
on the kitchen table, next to the jeweled case holding

21

her pack of Salem's. The warm musty smell of the wood paneled basement we'd have Christmas in, and the itchy elastic of my red jammies. The soft thump of my heels against the stairs as I'd run down to look at the train set. Me and my sister caught fireflies in the backyard around the hemlock trees, running through the wet grass in our Little Mermaid night gowns. We put them in a mason jar as a nightlight between our twin beds. I think about it now and each memory still feels, happy. Untarnished.

I can shut my eyes and do a panoramic of each room, down to the crocheted blankets on the back of their couch and the thick woven orange rug in front of the wood stove. But the abuse itself? Nothing but empty filing cabinets. The memories are never there when I go looking for them. Echoes of emotions have only begun appearing with time, like small children poking their heads out from hiding places, wondering if it's safe to come out.

What my childhood mind saved at the forefront, were statements that I couldn't quite understand, but filed away to register later. My mother was uncomfortably graphic about exactly what had and had not transpired. I still wanna turn my head away and wrinkle my nose remembering her leaning down to me in the hallway after a doctor's visit, "…they checked you out and you were too small for him to penetrate you."

I don't remember anything about the doctor's visit, but I'll never forget that. I didn't know exactly what her statement meant, but it made me sick every time she repeated it reassuringly. I'd catch bits and pieces from her speaking with family members and friends over the phone-

"…went to put Rebecca in her crib and it was wet. He'd ejaculated onto her blanket… I know… can you believe it?"

"Rebecca was in her highchair, and we just laughed at her all night because she was eating with her eyes closed, she'd only open them to look down and grab food. Now we know it's because Charles was sitting directly in front of her at the table. I know…poor little Rebecca…"

I was told over and over, "Samantha's the one that was *really* abused. You're ok Rebecca, you're fine."

But what I heard was, "What happens to you doesn't count."

We used coloring books with giraffes sitting at the witness stand to teach us how to speak in a

23

courtroom. Our main therapist, Brenda, whom my mother became extremely close with, I later found out worked the Little Rascal's case, one of the most expensive child abuse and satanic ritual cases in North Carolina's history to date. She was animated and eccentric, I liked her, but even at that age I noticed she was oddly persistent on getting the answers she wanted. She was playful and lighthearted one minute, and then it was business the next.

My mom made sure we were always using correct terminology like "vagina" and "penis" and "bowel movement." Ya can't say "poop" in the courtroom.

(This may have bit her in the ass later when I ran up and down the beach like Paul Revere alerting the masses, "Be careful!!! Don't step on the jellyfish testicles!!!" Many lives were saved that day)

During all this, my dad was building a new home for us about ten minutes over the bridge. The plastic was still hanging over the windows of my freshly painted purple bedroom, when I broke down with guilt the night before the trial.

"Hey Mom, remember that story I told you and Brenda, about Grandma walking up on Charles trying to mess with me on the swing?"

24

"Yes Rebecca… " she said with a tone of impending disappointment.

"I made it up. I'm sorry. "

"Thank you for telling me Rebecca," frowning and sighing as she left the room.

Her quick exit and the look on her face made me cry even harder. I was no longer of use. I'd done the right thing and told the truth, and it only disappointed her. I remember thinking, "Now I've done it. They're gonna lose the whole case tomorrow because of me. Miss Brenda's gonna be so mad."

Every therapy session had ended when I said what someone wanted to hear. I was hugged when I praised my mother and stayed quiet unless spoken to. I was applauded and brought laughter when I made derogatory statements about men. I eventually made up the lie to *really* make everyone proud of me. And they were! They commended me for speaking up and being so brave, but now I'd blown it. They wouldn't be proud of me anymore.

I remember gripping to my dad's rough hand as we stood to leave after the sentencing. Grandma Fran spun around, looking him square in the eye, "You bastard. Go to hell! "I remember wondering why she yelled at him and not my mom. My mom was the one that had pressed charges. He'd been busy building the house throughout all of it. I don't remember anything else from that day except that moment, but from what I've gathered, Charles plead guilty to all charges and was restricted from crossing the state line.

Months after the trial ended, we'd come down the stairs of our new house to Mom anxiously waiting with a pitiful frown. The kitchen table would be covered with sharpie markers, scissors, and pajamas we'd worn to Fran and Charles'. Lookin' like a *real* depressing surprise party.

"Girls I know you're upset, so we're gonna cut up these pictures and you write or draw anything you want on these shirts and then we'll cut 'em up! You just be as angry as you want!"

But all I really wanted to do was eat a peanut butter 'n marshmallow sandwich and watch *Pee-Wee's Playhouse* in my plastic bejeweled high heels. (Cowboy Curtis later went on to become Morpheus... What I'm sayin' is, I feel like he 'n I have come a long way together.)

Our family photo albums looked like they'd been vandalized. Pages full of scribble marks, blacked out dates, and empty holes where Charles' face used to be. Our little hands holding onto a headless figure in front of a majestic sunset. All of this erased nothing, it only highlighted the fact that there'd been a major catastrophe in our family. *Everything* went back to the abuse, every bad mood, every stomach ache; constantly reminding us we'd be permanently crippled by this event. It became our mom's life purpose and obsession to raise awareness and discuss its lasting effects.

Now, this is where I understand some people reading this might say, "What's wrong with your life's purpose to be fighting injustice? Especially if it's happened to your own children? " I hear that, but this is where being extremely empathic and sensitive can get *real* disorienting. Where we may begin shaming ourselves, wondering why we get these horrible feelings, red flags, and "bull shit." messages. Especially about people we love and admire.

The times that no matter how praised the individual, no matter how righteous the cause, we can't ignore this inner alert, "Something just feels…off. Why do they have to scream *so* loud? What is it they don't want me to see?"

It ain't for nothin.

Every April our house was nothing but boxes of blue ribbons, straight pins, and monotonous buzzing and clicking as the copying machine spit out papers to be stuck to anything around town that would stand still. Things like, "The Only Smack Your Kid Ever Needs," with a set of lips turned diagonally at the corner.

She also got involved opening a child abuse prevention and counseling center. There were fundraising golf tournaments and fashion shows to organize, and then the actual counseling sessions we went to constantly. I don't think I ever made it through a full week in elementary school without getting picked up to go somewhere, but no matter how many things she brought me to, she seemed constantly aggravated by my presence.

"Rebecca!" she'd hiss under her breath, shooing me away from her skirt to continue her conversation. I didn't know where else it was she wanted me to go exactly, so I'd take two steps back to give her space and try not to cry. I learned how to read exactly what I felt off of the adults in the room, to be the best people pleaser I could. If they liked me, they'd tell my mom how much they liked me, and then my mom would feel proud of herself and kinda parade us around. *Then* she wouldn't shoo me away or reprimand me for crying again.

Inside most days, I was silently screaming. Too anxious to regularly attend most of my classes with all the other kids, I acquired a paralyzing fear of vomiting specifically. If I could make it through the day, it was through a cold sweat and swallowing profusely in a state of panic. I clung to my teachers, using the same tactics I did to get along with my mother's friends, trying my best to appear like their equal rather than a silly child. The bustling, rigid, and competitive environment at school, being corrected and watched all the time, it terrified me. I smiled and did my best, but some days I was inconsolable. I'd grip the handles of the car on the way to school crying and screaming, "Please don't make me go. Please!!!" I remember her calling my dad at work one morning as I sobbed in the kitchen, "Do you hear this Daniel?! Do you hear her?! You wanna come home and deal with your daughter?"

When my friends would circle around on the playground, usually a group of five, I'd silently count out three of us, reminding myself three out of five children are molested, so that meant I wasn't the only one. I spent a lot of kindergarten into fourth grade having lunches with the school counselors and eating my snacks with the nurse. Every day was a struggle. Every day was dragging my feet through quicksand.

I remember sitting with my back to the cafeteria lunch line as the register beeped and students slid their trays along. Chairs squeaked and I was pulling my honey and peanut butter sandwich from my lunch bag. My friends sat around me talking, but I was checked out in my own mind. I saw a flash of how men and women's genitals fit together, and then it was gone. I thought about it later in the auditorium as we sat for a show that afternoon, "Is that…really what happens? " I thought. We'd discussed anatomy and good touch bad touch plenty through the years, but never how boys and girls had sex. For obvious shameful reasons, I told no one.

I felt alone and isolated much of the time, like something was terribly wrong with me and everyone could see it, but I didn't wanna be pitied or laughed at, I stayed quiet and shy and well behaved until I could go home and escape back into my own imagination. That was my constant throughout my childhood. The one place that didn't shoo me away or tell me to stop crying. Not much of what I saw made sense, but what I couldn't see, what I could *feel*, was pretty clear. I was fine being alone and entertaining myself, but night time was a different story. I could never sleep over at friend's houses, night time just didn't feel safe.

The setting sun always felt like water rising in a locked room, everyone else was fine while my senses became deafening. I felt like I couldn't escape this impending doom that rang through my ears and screeched down the hallways. I had to get outside to breath, to get a break from the buzzing. I'd push the screen door open to the front porch and feel my ribs expand. It felt like someone was just slowly cranking the volume higher and higher in my head.

I'd lie in bed, rolling the texture of the night between my teeth, chewing on it and clenching my jaw til I could bite down on it between my back molars. I could feel the humming of the hallway light in my cheeks and the weight of it on my tongue.

"What is this?" I'd think. "What am I feeling? Is there a name for this? How does everyone else just… go to sleep?"

I hated the hallway to my parent's room, I'd get chills every time I walked down it on the way to the bathroom. It felt like something was always waiting for me, an awful feeling that had become frozen right between my room and theirs. I'd end up going downstairs and wandering the house, sleeping on the porch until the sun came up. Some mornings I'd be so rattled from the hours of white knuckling my blanket and gritting my teeth, I'd finally get physically ill and throw up from exhaustion.

I'd sit on the hammock swing, leaning my head against the cool chain and holding onto the braided ropes thinking, "You're ok, you're ok, you made it, it's day time now. You made it. "

My mom didn't understand why I was so afraid of getting sick, so I made up another lie I knew she'd go along with. I told her I kept imagining Charles crawling up to my window with a ladder. She ate it up with a spoon sayin', "Oh Rebecca!!! It's ok!"

I'd had stomach bugs off and on for years and been completely fine, so I myself had no idea why I was living in such a state of panic and impending doom at the thought of vomiting, even more so, the thought of no one *helping me* when it happened. This story about Charles at least made sure that my mom would be on call in case I *did* throw up.

Throughout my life it's continued. If someone or something exhausts me, makes me feel uneasy, or drains me, I've often just gotten a cold or extreme nausea so I have a *real* reason to avoid the situation. When I push aside my emotions or feelings, afraid to rock the boat or sound completely nuts, I've subconsciously manifested something physical to *prove* something's wrong. To assure everyone and myself I'm not just being too sensitive. To make sure someone realizes I'm in distress.

I'd always had imaginary friends and wild visions, but the paranormal activity in our house progressively got less fun and playful. It just seemed to get more and more scary and outspoken. I talked to my angels and God constantly since I can remember, but the boisterous and unnerving stuff... *that* I could've gone without. That's the thing with being sensitive, we don't just feel or see one side of things, we see 'em all. So the supernatural, paranormal, whatever you wanna call it, is often pretty normal for many of us. It's realizing it's *not* considered normal for others that often makes us go quiet, especially when we've been called crazy, or delusional for years. Most of us have spent so many sleepless nights fighting it all alone simply because no one would listen.

CHAPTER THREE

"I've been to every single book I know
trying to soothe the thoughts that plague me
so."

Be Still My Beating Heart

Sting

Once I started middle school, Samantha quickly became my mother's new best friend. They were constantly whispering to each other and giggling at the house. Always reminding me how awkward I was, especially when it came to boys. They'd started going out of town for their own private counseling sessions once a month. Their new therapist had a home office a couple hours away.

Jealoooooous! Whoa buddy was I jealous. After much pleading and whining on my part, I was finally allowed to tag along a couple times, but only under the agreement that I wait in the car outside, and just listen to my Motown tapes. Not a problem. I just didn't wanna be left behind, I was desperate to be included, so much in fact, I opened myself to the inevitable bullying that came after every one of their sessions.

Lanette Sibo, their therapist, was an abrasive opinionated woman with ferocious red hair that stood straight out from her temples, like a flight attendant pointing to the emergency exits on either side of the cabin.

"So *you're* daddy's little girl huh," sizing me up, looking for a wire under my Delia's t-shirt, "you tell him everything don't you?" Her voice intimidated me almost as much as her broad shoulders and thick Irish accent.

"Oh! She's her father's keeper, that's for sure." Mom chimed in, "she just thinks he can do no wrong," And the three of them would shake their heads at me sighing in disgust.

Tough crowd.

I idolized my dad, I ran to him for sanctuary, clinging to his pant leg and holding his calloused hands tightly. He didn't seem to be around for the most part during the therapy sessions and court preparations, so with him, none of that had to be brought up every fifteen minutes. He worked hard and was gone most of the day, but I was waiting at the door for him every evening once I heard his truck coming through the neighborhood. Smelling of diesel fuel and wet sand from digging ditches all day, he'd put his wallet away in his cubby, slide his boots off and pour his pocket change into the drawer, same as every night before. I'd try and hang onto him as long as I could before he headed upstairs to the office.

I'd sit up there for hours at the computer desk behind him while he sorted through bills and payroll, just wanting to be near him. If he was building something, staining something, welding something, fiber glassing something, I wanted to learn how to do it or at least how it worked. I spent most of my weekends just following him around, handing him tools and asking what things were called and what they were for.

"See now this, is called a tapered bore. See how it makes those tiny curled metal shavings?"

He taught me to meticulously measure out resins and glues, "See how ya wanna stir it slowly, mixing from the bottom and pulling upward? We wanna make sure we don't stir too quick. We want the least amount of air pockets and bubbles we can." I thought he was the smartest man alive.

Our lunch breaks were always A&W Root Beer, PBJ's, and barbecue chips. He taught me how people find passion and fulfillment through hard work. The reward of doing things you've never done before, and figuring it out along the way. He is forever rebuilding boat motors, digging out septic tanks, and rewiring electrical systems.

I came home from school for Christmas break one year, to see him smiling ear to ear, flipping through the channels on the television. He'd installed a satellite dish weeks before, that quickly proved to be a mistake, and we were so sad we wouldn't be able to watch *A Christmas Story* marathon. "MERRY CHRISTMAS!" He yelled and laughed. "How? What?" I yelled. He just smiled at me, looked at our neighbor's back yard, and gave a wink. They were out of town for the holidays, and being the ditch digger he was, he simply dug their cable up so we could borrow it for a couple days. The fact that the neighbor happened to be my French teacher made it even better.

He may not have made a lot of time for us, and to be completely honest, he gave it freely to everyone *but* us. Volunteering to do favors for coworkers and church members, or suddenly needing to go tracking with the Mormon missionaries at the last minute. Most of our standing appointments were cancelled simply by his turning up absent. I never planned for him to be at any volleyball games or even know many details about my life or what grade I was in. It made it easier when our mom pointed out how much he didn't care, or that he didn't even know how old both of us were, I could just tell myself, "Well I never *asked* him to. It doesn't matter, he's busy, he's got more important things to worry about."

Besides, every once in a while, he *would* set aside time just for me, skipping out on work so we could go fishing. None of the forgotten plans or birthdays mattered once we were on the water. Everything was forgiven, I knew he loved me, he just had more important things to take care of most the time. I understood his time was precious and I should be grateful when he shared it with me rather than nag him.

This made me an easy target for disgust from my mom and sister, and so I just clung to him even harder.

It wasn't that he was the one to sit up with me every night when my panic attacks were at their worst, but he was the only one that I'd listen to. I needed to hear *him* say that it was all in my mind, and that the fear was all in my head. Whatever he said, I believed. It was all just awful nightmares, my mind playing tricks on me. I just needed to get a handle on myself, stop making myself crazy.

But every night, the cold sweats hit, my throat tightened, and it just started all over again. No matter where I slept, it found me. The noises, the nightly visitors, the overwhelming nausea. I'd finally fall asleep curled up on the couch downstairs and wake up to pounding footsteps running toward me, talking and laughter in the corners of the room. One night I gripped the blanket tight as I could, squeezing my eyes shut as a metal scraping sound grew louder and louder, until it was ringing in my head. It sounded as if someone had picked up the shovel we used for getting ashes out of the wood stove, and was furiously scraping it along the brick taunting me. Faster, faster, and faster until I finally sat straight up, turning to face them, but no one was there. It was always as if someone was cranking the volume higher and higher until my heart could leap from my chest, and when I'd finally turn to face them, there was nothing.

This blaring truth was always just out of my reach, slipping away just when I was ready to catch it. I could never quite put my finger on why the house felt haunted, why I was fighting a battle no one else could see. I reprimanded myself constantly, reminding myself it was only me doing this, but that didn't stop my jaw from clenching or my stomach from tying itself in ropes. I felt completely separate from the life my physical body was living, imagining a world of wonder and joy, while my insides screamed from the top of a cliff.

No one else around me seemed to be having a paralyzing problem, just me. I tried to fix the isolation I felt, by making everyone around me get along. If something looked off or one of my parents did something hurtful, I was quick to make an excuse so everyone else would let em off the hook.

While I was still in the fourth grade, Beverly, or Bev as most everyone called her, (my mom) wasn't working at the time, and I'd gotten pretty upset when she wasn't in line to pick me up after school. The assistants invited me inside to call her from the front desk, but even after four calls, she hadn't answered.

"Honey, should we call a family member or do you know of a friend's mom nearby who could take you home?"

I was scared something had happened. Where else could she be? I also didn't wanna admit maybe she'd just forgotten about me. I was on the brink of tears, "She's coming! I remember now, I think she said she was going to the store." Mmmm not true.

I walked back out and waited at the flag pole as the last mini-van zoomed into the parking lot. It was approaching five o-clock. Our assistant principal (who we were all fucking *terrified* of) offered me a ride home.

"We'll have to walk a few blocks to Good Year Tire though," she said, "my car's in the shop."

We walked down the sidewalk as cars passed and I *prayed* no one saw us. It was bad enough kids had asked how I already knew our D.A.R.E officer when he first came to school. He'd been one of our officers during the court trials.

I walked in the door, hearing Dr. Phil's voice twanging from our living room,

"Mom?"

"Yeah Rebecca."

"Um… you didn't pick me up. I called four times from the front office…"

"Oh is it already 3-o-clock!? Oh darlin' I'm sorry. Mommy must've gotten side tracked."

"…but your show *starts* at 4."

"Rebecca! I said I'm sorry!"

The living room had stacks of legal pads with bullet notes and exclamation points. Underlined sentences that summed up her childhood and described her unfulfilling marriage. She scavenged for newspaper cut outs and quotes, tacking them along the walls and hanging cork boards for her larger collections, making the laundry room look like a conspiracy theorists studio apartment. Any missed appointments or disregard for time seemed to be quickly justified or simply not recognized all together.

I'm so scared sometimes as a grown woman, wanting to have kids of my own, that I'm doomed to repeat this.

I journal religiously, and have for the last fifteen years. I look at my stacks of beautifully bound booklets and spiral notebooks, and I'm terrified I'll leave my children standing at the flag pole. That my most extravagant dinner will be nachos. That they'll cry to me to please hold their hand and I'll push them away. That I'll be distracted, wound up in my own self-validation. I worry something that's supposed to be extremely healthy and empowering like journaling, may one day make my children suspect I'm "losin' it." That they'll grow up with a mother who is self- obsessed and neglectful.

I have to remind myself to hold my head up. Shoulders back. It's ok to feel good about myself, to have pride in myself, to deeply understand myself. That there's a difference between being self-obsessed, and self-aware. And I'll *just have* to keep saying it until my head no longer feels the need to bow. Until I learn taking care of myself doesn't mean I'm abandoning people I love. Until I stop crying when a five course candle lit meal isn't waiting for my husband everyday he gets home, apologizing to him for failing once again. I see the look in his eyes and I know I'm reaching for expectations he never placed on me. And he knows, I'm still trying to receive love from someone who's never had it to give. He puts his arms around me and lets me cry again.

Every time I've fucked up, spoken up, questioned actions, shown emotion, my father's quick to say, "Ya know that's just your mother talkin'." And I feel my head become heavy.

I feel as though I've failed. I've done everything I can to escape it, to be someone he'd be proud of, easy to love, and yet I've somehow come back around to the very thing I've been running from. I've become the person he's always despised, the person who ruined his life. I'm just as crazy as the rest of em.

No matter whose side I clung to growing up, eventually, I failed them. I became the enemy. I wasn't allowed to hear details or plans on anything for fear I'd blow their cover. "She's the stand in wife." my mother would say to others constantly, referring to my close relationship with my dad. Why'd she have to say it like *that,* it made me wanna vomit every time. And she said it a *lot.*

The harder I clung to my dad and spent as much time with him as I could, the worse I got it from the two of them. Whispering to one another and side eyeing me, tallying how many bowls of cereal I'd had that day, how silly my makeup looked, how shy and uncomfortable I was. They'd send Sam's male friends downstairs to find me, telling them I had huge crushes on them. I was mortified.

Mom approached me in the kitchen one day like a bully,

"So, me and your sister have been talking, and you're *definitely* high maintenance."

I didn't even know what exactly that meant, but she made it clear that her and Sam were *not.* They were low maintenance, and boys like low maintenance.

If I did well, if I got attention, it wasn't received well, I always ended up apologizing. Even if it was art projects, I was praised and then reminded how bad it made those in my family *without* artistic talent feel. I stopped sharing a lot, not wanting to risk my excitement being poked and prodded. I locked myself in my room for days in sixth grade, working on a poster for a contest at school. I played the song *Bosnia* by *The Cranberries* over and over again, sobbing over this poster board. I'd drawn a young girl in her jammies, alone, holding her doll in the middle of the street amongst crumbling buildings and rubble.

"*This* is art." I thought to myself.

That was the first time I remember becoming completely engulfed in emotions. I was intoxicated in this deep sorrow and grief, for what I didn't even know, but it was pouring out of me, and I felt vulnerable bringing it into school. I remember the teacher handing back the judged posters weeks later and I slumped in my desk as I saw the green ribbon, *Honorable Mention*.

"They didn't even get it." I thought, "All that crying, Dolores O'Riordan must be exhausted…and for an honorable mention… I bet somebody won with a damn beach scene. Some seagulls 'n dolphins or some shit. People love damn beach scenes…they don't get it."

There'd been so much I felt and experienced that no one else saw or at least seemed to understand. Aside from the house being haunted, there were constant synchronicities and messages from my spirit family throughout the days that no one else seemed to acknowledge. A whole world I felt like no one else was seeing. Again I felt isolated, like I was living in a story all my own. I felt like I was tuned in to a totally different radio station.

My sister, her friend, and I were out in the back yard playing on the rope sing, twisting it as high as we could, then running and jumping to spiral faster and faster. They'd stepped away for a minute as I was taking my turn, and accidently flew off the swing toward the pine trees. I remember seeing the bark on the tree I was quickly approaching, and then in the next second, being placed gently on the ground with my legs crossed in front of me. I jerked my head left and right making sure I was awake.

"Did you guys SEE THAT?" I yelled, but they hadn't. I spent the rest of the day trying to figure out how I went from heading face first toward that tree, to floating down and sitting on the pine straw like a damn snowflake. I mean I knew I had some angels lookin' out for me, but that was the first time I'd seen a full on interception.

My imagination had no shortage of opportunities to flourish growing up. My sister, my cousin and I, spent days shooting movies with our old video camera. Lugging around the attached VCR and setting up the tripod so we could have all three of us in the shot at once (usually during our Jerry Springer episodes…) My cousin and I would meet at the path between our neighborhoods, building sets and creating costumes as old witches or princesses. Hurricanes meant we'd be filming *The Today Show* for the next 48 hrs, using the fantastic footage to make authentic weather broadcasts. I happened to have the entire intro memorized, "LIIIIVE from studio 1A iiiiiin Rockefella Plazaaaa." So, it was pretty legit.

I sat on the edge of my bed one afternoon, now in the seventh grade, adjusting my thrift store blouse and smeared lipstick before our next Springer scene we were about to shoot. My sister came in asking the same question she'd been asking me for a month straight.

"Wouldn't you just *love* to live in the mountains?"

I tried to give her an answer that would satisfy her persistent inquisitions, cause obviously this question was keeping her up at night.

"I mean, I *do* love to visit the cabin in Pennsylvania… but I don't know that I'd want to *live* there. Like it's fun to visit the mountains, cause it's not all the time, but like, I like it here. Why do you keep askin'?"

"Just wondering," she grinned.

About a week later, I was sitting in class when the phone rang and my teacher turned to me and said, "Rebecca your dad's here to pick you up."

He is? Sweeeeeeet!

The crash of my locker door echoed down the empty hallway and I bounced my backpack on my shoulders rounding the corner to the front office. I got to the double doors expecting to see the boat hitched to his truck out front, but there he stood, dressed in slacks and a tie. Not dressed for fishing at all. My chest tightened.

"What's up? I thought you were pickin' me up to go fishin'…"

Ignoring my statement, he thanked the ladies at the front desk and turned to me, "You got all your stuff?"

"Yeah."

The clack of his shoes against the tile broke the silence as he pushed opened the double doors. I never liked that sound, his Sunday loafers. That sound means business, 'n it's never really been good business from my experience. That sound means funeral, church, or court.

"Dad?"

He opened the door for me to climb in the truck and I slung my backpack on the floorboard, buckling myself in and starting to hyperventilate. Still not saying a word, he started the engine and took a left at the stop sign toward the south end of the island, the opposite direction of our house.

"Dad, did somebody die?"

"No Rebecca, nobody died."

Still nothing.

I just stared at him as he squinted over the steering wheel, I could practically see the smoke coming off of him. We made it only a couple miles down the road before he made a sudden U-turn and started heading back in the opposite direction.

"Dad."

Nothing.

He parked at the house and we both climbed out of the truck completely silent, reverently walking inside so as not to disturb whatever it was we weren't discussing.

"Rebecca I need to talk to you about something."

"Ok."

"Your mother is taking you girls and moving to Buena Vista Virginia in a month, and there's not a damn thing I can do about it."

"What?" I started sobbing, "She can't just take us away like that!"

"Rebecca. I've tried to tell you! Her and your sister have been scheming and planning this for months! *Months* Rebecca! You see how evil and twisted your mother is?" Jabbing his index finger into his temple, "I've been trying to tell you this whole time, but you're gonna see just how evil she is now! She's gonna take you girls from me and I can't do a damn thing about it."

We both just sat and cried with our head in our hands.

Then I got it.

51

Oh. The fucking mountains…

CHAPTER FOUR

"You say it all depends on the money, 'n
who is in your family tree."
Bloody Well Right
Supertramp

*W*e arrived in Buena Vista on Halloween, and
by Thanksgiving break, I was packing my little suitcase
to go home with my dad and never come back. I played
nice, I did my best to join in my mom and sister's
excitement for a new start and new friends, but I
sincerely fucking hated it. I wouldn't even attend
school the first week we were there in protest. I was
miserable.

My dad had fallen asleep while I was on the
phone with him one night and I went into absolute
hysterics. We called a relative down the street to check

on him, and they found him fast asleep with the cordless phone on his chest. He'd recently gotten a prescription for sleeping pills and dozed off mid conversation, but that was <u>it</u> for me, *someone* had to go home and take care of him. I remember my mom trying to console me, but becoming upset herself after seeing how distraught I was at the thought of losing him.

She'd become even more emotionally vacant the past months, not just from me, but in general. I'd come home from my last day at school before our move to Virginia, and didn't hear the tick of our dog Benny's nails against the wood floor. I looked around for him, mom was bagging utensils out of the kitchen drawers.

"Mom, where's Benny? Is he at the vet's?"

"I had him put to sleep this morning."

"What?"

"He's too old to make the trip Rebecca."

And that was it. She never mentioned it again. She never even looked up from rummaging through the drawers. She'd had him since I was a kid.

When Dad picked me up for the holidays, we made a vacation out of the trip home. Stopping at outlet malls to pick out new lamps and tables for the house. We needed rugs and dinnerware and blinds. We got home and hung fly fishing rods and nets over the fireplace. I hadn't told him yet that I wanted to stay for good, but we were already making the house our own.

I felt like this was it, our family could finally make a fresh start. No more nonstop therapy visits. No more screaming and fighting and bullying, no more suspicions of whose side someone was on or what they were scheming. I was a smart kid, but I'd never actually *tried* in school. I'd stopped handing in my homework as early as the fourth grade. I just didn't give a shit. I had more important things to worry about than fractions and reading assignments, so I ended up making school extremely stressful and hard on myself. While my sister was a straight A student, I was regularly making thirty-sevens on tests and quizzes. I wanted to make a new start, it was gonna be me 'n Dad now. Things would smooth out.

But it didn't last long.

We got word they both had come to town for Christmas, and would be in the neighborhood visiting family. "We almost made it," I thought, "It was almost over."

I remember both my parents crying in the kitchen, she'd agreed to come back home, he'd drive and help pick up all our things the next week. I was relieved and cautious all at once, I knew it wouldn't last. I knew the other shoe would drop eventually. We almost made it out.

A month later, I sat fidgeting and sipping water in a small office. Re-situating myself as the itchy couch cushions imprinted their woven pattern on the back of my legs from the sticky summer heat. I felt comfortable in this therapist's office. I liked that she sat out from behind her desk as we spoke, leveling the playing field. I was fifteen when I first started coming to see her, and once again, I didn't exactly know what I was supposed to get out of our sessions, except that my mom was waiting outside so… here I was.

On this day in particular, after multiple visits, and private discussions with the other members of my family, I think she'd gotten a better understanding of where I was. We'd moved on from talking about me, to life in general. Following a lull of silence and me quietly tugging at my shorts, she cleared her throat,

"Ya know, I want you to remember this Rebecca. An insane person will *never* question their sanity."

She paused looking at me, waiting for the lightbulb to spark. I just nodded agreeably, as if I clearly saw where she was going with this.

I didn't.

I just thought to myself, "Well, I must be extremely sane, because I question my sanity multiple times a day…" She sat in silence waiting for me to say something, but I just sipped more water from my little paper cup, tucking my shoulders up toward my ears.

Although we talked about mental health and daily stresses of individuals in general, it never occurred to me that I was there to possibly shed light on *anything* other than my own problems, make peace with *my own* faults, *my own* mistakes, and come to terms with how I've continuously made my own life difficult and seen things incorrectly.

So much of the insight that came from counseling sessions wasn't actually from anything that was said, but feeling someone recoil and release heavy exhales at my downplay of hurtful remarks or instances with family members. It wasn't until days and weeks later, I'd replay the therapist's reaction and think, "Did I say something wrong? Was that situation *not* what I thought?"

My mom had picked this woman to counsel the whole family after her and Sam had moved back home. She went through therapists like some women go through purses or shoes. She always said she was trying to sort things out and heal their marriage, but as soon as she didn't get the answers she wanted, it was onto the next office. The fact we were all seeing the same woman also made it impossible for me to get a clear reading from her on anyone in the family. That whole ethics thing. Hence the cryptic words of advice that didn't make sense til years later.

I was still up every night, spending most my time outside talking to God. The connection and support I felt from my spirit family had always been palpable, they were constantly surrounding me, unwavering. I'd rocked my dad to sleep when he was sobbing one night over Mom leaving, I felt responsible for his happiness. I always wanted to rely on my parents, but I knew I couldn't. I always knew they were reaching for something they'd never gotten, trying to fill a hole they had long before I was born. I think I started leaning heavily on the unseen safety net in the spirit world before I had a chance to realize it.

I think many of us do that with trauma, we don't question what it is that brings us stability and peace, we just hold onto it. Then as we get older we may question the very validity of unseen forces, the spirit realm, angels, ancestors, guardians, because everything else in life has shown us that love's only temporary.

That everyone leaves.

CHAPTER FIVE

"Why you act crazy. Not an act maybe."

I Stay Away

Alice In Chains

*M*om moved out again not long after that. Restraining orders were put in place, and she had to have a police escort to pick me up from the house. Things hadn't just fallen apart again, they exploded. I attended their court hearings, I wanted to see what was *really* going on. I sat far in the back, and the judge kept her eyes on me as the lawyers read out credit card statements and logged violations. I nodded my head yes or no, cueing the judge in on inaccurate or false statements.

My father had started seeing a woman from church, which that in itself didn't really bother me, but the extreme secrecy and his reluctance to divulge *any* information whatsoever? *That* bothered me.

She'd been brought around the family months prior, an extremely quiet woman, and he'd been quite hesitant about telling me who it was he was getting dressed up for in the evenings. I was excited he was getting back out there, but he continued with this unnecessary sneaky attitude, lying for no reason.

I was getting angry. I started seeing how much both of them had lied constantly, about anything and everything, about things I shouldn't have had to interrogate my own parents about.

So there I sat in that courtroom, pissed. Nodding my head emphatically, "LOCK EM UP!" The attorney read out the statements from a weekend trip, questioning where my father had gone and who he'd taken with him. He chuckled with a smug look, having no problem telling them the same thing he'd tell me,

"That's really none of your business."

They continued, inquiring about large payments made to The Church Of Jesus Christ of Latter-Day Saints. Again, he just laughed to himself, seeing it as another opportunity to make fools out of everyone attacking him. "That's my fire insurance." He stated, feeling quite satisfied with himself.

The judge looked right at me and I rolled my eyes, shaking my head. He was talking about his regular tithing paid to the church, insinuating that the lawyers and everyone present better do the same and get right with the Lord so they don't burn.

I wanted to believe that this wasn't *really* who they were. I wanted to believe that the divorce had just brought out the worst in them. That they had always brought the worst out in each other. They could not have *always* been pathological liars like this, I'd just caught em at a bad time. For the last fifteen years.

The angst was perfect timing though, as I was a sophomore in high school and at the peak of my salt. I'd somehow managed to scrape by my freshman year, still not handing in assignments and barely passing. My psychological and emotional bank account at that point was seriously overdrawn. Purgatory personified. It felt like I was reading the same book, but on a completely different chapter than everyone else my age.

I was already way past exhausted, I wasn't about to take instruction from anyone else.

I tried to let my teachers down easy when they met me, hinting that they may not actually see my face all that much.

"Oh my gosh, you're *Samantha's* sister! What a treat!" they'd exclaim, shaking their clipboard, "Oh she was just one of my favorite students!"

"Yeah she is great, she *is* great…"

This is usually when their smile began to fade as they slowly realized my short hair was coated in a week's worth of wax, I was holding no books, and there was more often than not, a fresh Hot Pocket stain visible somewhere on my person.

(When sharing this segment with a childhood friend, he made sure to critique, "Don't leave out the part about you spraying your clothes with Febreeze and blow drying the wrinkles out. That was your signature move." It sure was bud.)

Unlike me, Samantha wore strappy platforms and pencil skirts, and *never* with Hot Pocket stains. I on the other hand, was living the equivalent of wearing a Snuggie to a bar in your twenties. "Here to drink and do crosswords. Not interested in fellowship."

Staying true to my word, I went to school about every tenth day, just enough to stay on the roster for attendance, and not get kicked out of the house. I'd made a new best friend, Beth, when both of us dawning sunglasses, greasy hair, and bad attitudes, had raised our heads simultaneously and yelled at a fellow student,

"SHUT THE DOOR," as she made her usual late entrance to class. She and my childhood friend Veronica (Vern) became my new support group, and my God, did they have a lot to support.

These years were not filled with my proudest moments to say the least, it was definitely what some would call, a dark night of the soul. Which, happened to shine quite a light on the lack of responsibility I was taking for my own life. I'd never gotten my driver's license because that involved staying two hours after school for the course, and that would require I actually attend school regularly. And we all know by now, *that* wasn't gonna happen. I had Hot Pockets to eat, Fiona Apple CDs to play repeatedly, and Camel Lights to chain-smoke.

Booked solid.

Vern had started dating a fella named Marvin, who was living with five other men about forty-five minutes away in a dilapidated beach cottage. They were there illegally, working construction and sending money home to their families. On first coming to the house and meeting everyone, I thought, "Uhhh this is a lil sketch… I dunno Vern…" but the guys were really funny and nothing but nice, so maybe not so bad. All they wanted to do was drink, make us food, and buy us cigarettes.

Mmmmm… ok! I'll allow it.

Having no money at the time but the change I scrounged around the house and cashed in, I was rolling my own tampons out of toilet paper (it's insane just how many women have perfected this art when being strapped for essentials #hardknockcooterclub), and living off shared 7-11 coffee and cigarettes most the time. It's not that there wasn't food at home, but I was just trying to avoid being there as much as possible.

By this point, the deal I'd made with my dad to drop out at sixteen as long as I attended morning church seminary and completed my homeschooling, had proven to be another lost cause. It was tough to provide myself with adequate homeschooling when I was neither at home nor schooling.

Most mornings, I'd walk home as the rest of the local Mormon youth went on to school. Beth and Vern would pull up in the driveway later after walking out of math class, announcing they were, "Goin to have some pancakes!" I'd make us a big breakfast, we'd smoke a bowl, listen to some Incubus, maybe drive to Busch Gardens…really whatever we felt like doing for the day. If it was raining, we knew the guys would be home from work, so we'd head to the cottage. More often than not, the party had already started by the time we got there.

We'd walk in on a random Thursday to confetti covered tablecloths, streamers, and plastic champagne flutes. Handles of Capt. Morgan's, Coronas, cupcakes, cigarettes, and plates of cocaine assorted atop the table like a crack house Christmas party. *Mesa Qe Mas Aplauda* would be blaring from the stereo for the next twelve hours. This became the routine for weeks. And then months.

I remember seeing Cesar leaned up against the wall one night as we came in the front door; he hadn't slept in days. His face was pale and his eyes were red from the tears running down his cheeks. We begged him to go lay down, to eat some food and get some rest, we'd keep it quiet so he could sleep, but he shook his head no. I watched him do another bump and start crying even harder. That was the first time I started thinkin' maybe we weren't just havin' a good time anymore, but I also told myself, "Well I'm not like *that* though, I'm just dabbling…"

It made it slightly difficult to pump the breaks on my downward spiral of depression when the bad decisions were laid out for free with party streamers and cupcakes. I dunno if you've ever dabbled in coke, but for those of us *already* struggling with serious sensitivity and depression, it's just a splendid idea.

I say that sarcastically as in it is absolutely *not* splendid, unless self-loathing and melancholy for the three days following is your favorite. Which at the time, it *was* mine, so there-in lies the problem.

When it feels like a security blanket, and you want nothing more than to be buried under the covers day in and day out, it feels like home to pull self-destruction over your head, and turn out the lights. The days following long nights of partying usually entailed me chain smoking and listening to *Sour Girl* on repeat for the next seventy-two hours. Vern and Beth would drop by for coffee and cigs periodically and then I'd climb back into bed. Time kinda lurched in an uncoordinated fashion, the days were spliced together with long naps and crying spells.

(Side note. How *do* coke heads sniff out other coke-doers so well? Shouldn't their sniffing abilities, in fact, be impaired by the very activity itself? Years later I'd continue to be approached by people inquiring if I, "like to party." Lining up bumps on restaurant toilets before I even had a chance to deny their accusations. I didn't wanna offend anyone by not accepting their generous offers, but lesson learned. Offend people. Turn em down left 'n right. Take care of your damn nasal cavities.)

We'd been at the beach cottage regularly for months, when a cop car followed me and Vern into the guys' driveway as we returned from our coffee and cigs run. Cocky little shits we were, we lit out cigarettes before acknowledging him, then stepped out of the car nonchalantly asking him what was up.

"You girls really shouldn't be hanging out here. This isn't a good place."

"Oh I get it, cause they're Mexicans 'n we're white girls? Mmhm, thanks for the warning. Is there something we're *actually* doing wrong officer?"

"You didn't have your headlights on when you came across the street."

Oh suck on a lemon dude, it's barely dusk. He was obviously waiting for a reason to pull us over. We just stared at him impatiently, holding our plastic bags of Frappuccinos and Camel Lights, blinking our eyelids as loud as possible.

"I'm gonna tell you girls one more time, you don't need to be around here."

He handed Vern a business card, ya know, just in case we wanted to call him later to grab a beer or somethin'. His tires crackled over the gravel as he pulled back onto the side street, and we puffed away, examining his card.

Detective Jonathan L. Smithers; with "**Johnny**" in bold, centered in quotations after his full name. This entertained us to no end.

"He has his fuckin' nickname on his CARD!? Ohhhh this is too good…"

"STOP IT!" I cackled, coughing smoke and s'mores flavored coffee all over myself.

"You can call me Johnny, cause I'm a keeeeeewl cop."

"What a fuckin' tool… Yeah thanks for the wise words Johnny! Way to be a racist asshole Johnny!"

Welp, tool bag or not… Johnny *was* tryin' to give us a legitimate heads up. It's too bad we got so tickled at his business card we disregarded any of the advice. Sorry Johnny.

The reality of the situation we were involved in started coming into focus after that. There were incidents that at the time, were quite comical to us, (on account of the complete denial and superfluous rum I have no doubt.) but nonetheless, things started lookin' a lil sketch.

We came back to the house from a dance party around 3am, to see a scrappy lookin' woman standing in the living room, motionless and wide eyed. She was wearing an oversized Bob Marley t-shirt that hung from her shoulders like a wet blanket down to her scrawny knees and bare feet. It looked as if she'd ripped it off a clothes line, and just busted in the back door escaping the cops.

(In hindsight... this could have *actually* been how and why she came to possess that shirt.)

So here we come swinging the front door open singing, "DAME MAS GASOLIIIIIIINAAAAAAA-" We froze, having a silent stare down with this woman for a good five seconds. If she touched my Capt. Morgan's I swear to GOD!

She then snapped out of her paralysis, spun, and scuttled through the back bedroom, out of the house, and into the dark like a bony legged Rastafarian house roach.

We shrieked, "WHA!? WHO!? Y'all did we just get ROBBED!?"

"Girls don't worry bout it, don't worry, esta bien esta bien!" They repeated, coaxing us inside, completely sidestepping our apparent roach problem.

"Um yall. Who *was* that!? Nobody knows her!?"

"Si si, we know her, she mucho loco, mucho coca. Esta bien esta bien."

(Our Spanglish was in full swing at this point.)

"Ok well like, me no *know* her!! Me no like that shit!!"

Then a week or so passed and it was back to business as usual. Always keeping an eye out for policia, but nothing seemed to be out of the ordinary. But then a few nights later, the house roach was back.

This time she was parked outside, right off the main highway, honking her car horn and screaming at the top of her lungs at 2 in the morning, "I WANT MY EIGHT BALL!!!"

The guys were crawling around the house, turning off every light and dead bolting the doors. They had us crouched in a back bedroom to keep quiet and out of sight. This shit was serious. Unfortunately, at such a time as this, Vern and I had some serious church giggles. We were pretty toasted and could not control our laughter, watching these grown ass men crawling on all fours around the house frantically shushing one another.

I whispered to Vern, "Girl I feel like ANNE FRANK!" and we fucking *lost it*, rolling on the floor cackling and snorting.

I assure you, the guys did *not* find my joke as entertaining as we did.

"Y'all just don't get it. Y'all didn't do Accelerated Reader for some personal pan pizzas." We sassed, still laughing as they shot us silent looks to kill.

We had no idea what was actually going on in that house. That and we just didn't give enough of a shit to actually ask questions. We just kinda sat in it, self-defeating.

It reminded me of my mother coaxing me back to bed when I couldn't stop crying. Feverishly pinning mountains of blue ribbons, the copying machine clicking and spitting out posters, and me standing in the doorway of the office with swollen eyes.

"Rebecca, depression is awful. Your daddy's never believed me. Mommy understands, you don't need to go to school today, just get back in bed. I'll bring home some more Zoloft tomorrow."

That kinda love hugs you like a straightjacket.

It's comforting at first, calming to be held so tight, but then days have passed, and you're no longer sure if you have the strength to come out from under it.

71

That to me, is what the reasoning away of self-destruction is. Imitation love, poured on like mortar and wet sand. Just give it up kid, you were never gonna win anyway.

Things with my dad had become dangerously close to violent. We were having screaming matches daily, I knew I had driven him past his breaking point by then. The old boat he and I always fished on, sat on a trailer in the back yard now collecting leaves. I'd sit up there at night after my walks, high in the tower almost level with the tree line, and I'd look down at our house and cry, wondering how I'd ended up completely alone. I'd done everything I could.

I could feel my angels sitting right next to me, not saying a word, just assuring me I'd *never* be alone.

The pain I felt was so unbearable, the wee morning hours felt like the only time I could purge it. I'd wail and sob, sometimes so loud the neighbor's lights would come on. My father would storm on the porch demanding I shut up.

We both looked like ghosts, losing color and completely exhausted from the emotional battles every day. He glared at me one night, shaking as we fought, his hand was tightly gripping a chef's knife over the cutting board as I taunted him,

"What are ya gonna do HUH!?" Knocking a cookie tin across the kitchen to punctuate my threat. I had two whole flights of stairs to stomp away on, but it was just never enough. I'd grab a blanket and end up on the front porch swing, crying to my angels again, begging for guidance from the one source I'd never felt manipulate or shame me. I never received sugar coated answers, or messages of "light and love," but more so,

"We hear ya kiddo. Life can be intense, but keep going. Don't drown in the turmoil of your family, diving deeper trying to pull them to the surface. We are here, always. **We** are your family, we've got you."

I could feel their arms around me, a kiss on my forehead, or a soft grip on my hand. "We're right here." And I'd cry and lean my head against the unseen comfort, so tired.

I had no idea where my dad had gone, he was void of any emotion, anything even relevant to the protective hand I'd clung to my entire life. The man I'd rocked to sleep, and promised I'd never leave.

My mom had insisted time and time again she didn't feel safe before she left the second time. She just knew he was gonna shoot her. She threw one of his pistols into the cement mixer behind the house, and another one into the woods.

I started pushing him as far as I could. Begging for him to crack, for him to show some kind of emotion, *any* kind of emotion.

The screen door opened as I sat out there one evening, and he held the cordless phone out to me, "Beth's on the phone Rebecca."

I took a long drag off my cigarette, tapped the ash onto the porch, and exhaled slowly, "You can tell her I'll call her back." Come on mother fucker, do somethin'.

The reality was, I didn't hate him at all, I just really wanted him to think I did, so maybe he'd fight back, beg me to be his friend again. I'd run out of avenues. He was the only person in our family I'd *ever* really trusted, that I ever felt I could rely on. He was the only one I thought would never leave, and now he barely acknowledged my presence.

He was gone.

Everything had changed once the divorce became final. He didn't need me anymore. The game was over.

No matter how hard I cried, no matter how many letters I wrote him, pleading for him to just be my dad, he had already shut down.

"What do you *want* from me?" he'd say, shaking his head baffled at my outbursts, "I'm right here."

But he wasn't. I didn't know where he'd gone or why, but I couldn't reach him anymore. No matter how hard I tried.

CHAPTER SIX

"Such a strange numb, and it brings my
knees to the earth."

Minerva

Deftones

*W*hen my dad and I were still having our
nightly philosophical discussions, before I attended the
courtroom sessions and realized just how oblivious I'd
been, I asked him how things were going with Janice,
the woman from church he'd started seeing. I wanted to
be supportive and see him moving forward, but he
quickly assured me not to get too excited.

"OHHHHH no no no no, we're not dating. I'm
actually about to break things off so she doesn't start to

think we're dating. It's just nice to enjoy someone's company ya know, get out with other adults."

"Oh! Ok well yeah I mean, I wasn't tryin' to pry, I just, didn't know how it was goin'. Well cool, that's still good though, ya gettin' to socialize!"

"Yeah yeah no, it's nothing, she just doesn't really know anyone in town so…"

The very next night, I sat in the office while he typed in lotto tickets on the computer. He had his back to me, squinting at the numbers while I messed with post-it notes on his desk and asked how his day'd gone. He cleared his throat,

"I uh, I got somethin' to tell ya. But I don't know if you're gonna be excited, or mad."

"Welp uhh, why dontcha tell me, 'n then I'll tell ya which one it is," I laughed.

"Well, I uh, I proposed to Janice tonight."

He kept his back to me. The keyboard clicked as he peered over his glasses, careful to make sure he didn't miss those last three digits on the ticket.

Wait.

What?

"I… I thought… I mean didn't you just say last night y'all weren't even *dating*?"

He cleared his throat again and continued punching the keys, "Rebecca, I don't recall ever having that conversation."

I'm sorry.

Huh!?

He never turned around. He just kept clickin' those numbers into the computer.

I got up and walked outta the office. It felt like a grenade had just gone off inside my head.

And that was it.

From that moment, he was gone.

Shortly after their engagement, my sister and I stood sobbing in the church parking lot, begging him to spend just one more Father's Day with us. He scoffed and shook his head in disbelief,

"I already told you girls, Janice and I made plans to be at your Grandmother's. Either you can join us, or not."

Pain can shut us down in some crazy ways. In ways we can no longer see ourselves, not to mention anyone else. Whether it was triggered by the divorce, or had been under the surface all along and I hadn't seen it for what it was, I couldn't unsee it now.

We became total strangers.

Beth and Vern knew I was definitely *not* doing well, and they held onto me as tight as they could, but at the time, none of us were really rising to our potential so to speak. I mean, when ya have to steal toilet paper from the Walmart bathroom thinkin', "My God, if I get stopped for shoplifting this industrial size roll of toilet paper… not even a legit role meant for your home…"

Ya ain't really shootin' for the moon. Even if it's double ply.

For someone who always felt so deeply, I was terrified by how numb I was becoming. I couldn't make sense out of anything anymore. I started writing poetry to try and slough off the corrosion I felt steadily eating away at me. Squeezing my heart as hard as I could to see if I could still get anything out of it.

"… I'm tired 'n I wanna go home
This tide tugs at my soul
Dragging the bottom, grasping for sand
Only to be washed out again
Dark smoke stings, surrounding me
But it's all I have left to breathe
So I fill my lungs
Treading water 'til the next wave comes
I'm tired 'n I wanna go home…"

I was terrified my own light was gonna get snuffed out just like I'd seen everyone's in my family. It kept me even more addicted to swimming in my deepest emotions, isolating myself to dive deeper for fear my well was running dry.

I welcomed strong overpowering feelings, any kind of feeling, I didn't care if it felt dark or deceptive, so long as I kept feeling *something*. Emotions and energy became more palpable than anything else in everyday life. I made it through daytime in a sleepwalking state, waiting for the nighttime to come alive.

The nights were for my conversations with God and acknowledging the spirits walking alongside me. Some of them were comforting, while some of them felt like sludge that hung from my shoulders and tugged behind my feet. If I couldn't make sense of the waking world, I'd just try elsewhere.

I was a quarter mile from the bridge one night, when an outlined figure and a bright blueish white light collided with me abruptly. I jumped, frantically apologizing to the man, woman, whatever it was! In the startle, my arms shot out from my sides, flinging my phone out of my pocket. I knelt down, patting at the asphalt on my hands and knees, searching for my Nokia so I could shine a light down the bike path. I found it and quickly looked both ways up and down the trail, but there was no one. I'd yelped and tried to apologetically pat the shoulder… of no one.

Socially awkward in *all* dimensions and realities. Check.

I think the worst hitchhikers though, were always inside our home, waiting for me to climb into bed every night. The second my head hit the pillow, I'd feel the mattress press down behind me as a heavy figure curled up to my back. I'd let out a long exhale, here we go again. Then I'd roll over to see the same figure crouched in my closet, grinning as I acknowledged his presence.

They never left my side. Like those friends who love to dig at your doubts, make fun of you in public, and use your worst insecurities to crutch their own fractured spirit. Always laughing at your hurt feelings, "Oh come on, you know you love me," they chuckle devilishly.

They know you'll never have the guts to cut em off. To walk away. To say, "Alright. That's enough."

But at least you know you can always count on em to be there, through thick 'n thin, they'll always come back.

Like a planter's wart.

I was searching for escape, for validation, and I was startin' to scrape the bottom. I sat on our backyard swing late one night, the same swing my angels had plucked me from and placed me ever so gently on the ground years before. I gripped the ropes on either side of me tightly, and sent out a desperate plea for God to stop my heart from beating.

"Either stop this pain, or please just make my heart stop. I can't take this anymore. Years of this," I sobbed, "I can't do it."

Every time I'd thought things were finally gonna calm down, the dust would finally settle, there was just another explosion. Someone would drop another bomb. I was exhausted from trying to rebuild over and over and over again. It felt like the *humane* thing to do, after years of hanging on, would be to just have me divinely euthanized. I'd put in my time, had my fill, I'm beggin' ya coach, *please* just pull me outta the game.

Because of my usual experiences, I expected some huge reaction, a sudden darkness or chills to run through my body, but there was nothing. No beaming light, no sudden clarity or the meaning to life itself.

My tears just stopped, and I heard, "Rebecca just go to bed."

It was stern, but comforting. Like someone saying, "You're tired, move over 'n let me drive."

I stood up from the swing in a bit of a daze, walked inside, climbed the stairs to my room, and just laid there in silence.

It was that feeling before a hurricane makes landfall, knowing you've done everything you can, but the rest is out of your control. This eerie hot breeze starts blowing in off the ocean, and sea foam starts rolling in as the surf picks up. You look around you, studying details of all the homes and businesses you grew up with, not knowing if they'll still be standing later.

And you wait.

I heard my dad getting ready downstairs as the outlines of the trees became brighter, I still hadn't slept. He yelled up the stairs for me to wake up, and I asked him if I could talk to him for a minute. His feet sloughed up the carpeted steps and he sighed, aggravated that I was wasting time he was already running short on. He sat at the end of the bed,

"What is it Rebecca."

"Dad, I'm scaring myself. I'm having serious thoughts about hurting myself. I just, I think I need some help."

There. I said it. I got it out. Things are gonna be alright now.

He dropped his head. Understandably, I thought, this was a little much for him to hear from his youngest child, especially after the year he'd had. I felt bad for dropping such a bomb on him before he had to leave for work. I went to reach for his hand, to apologize for the bad timing, but then I realized he was shaking his head. His shoulders were jumping up 'n down.

He was laughing at me.

My stomach sank through my mattress.

"Rebecca…. Ya need to stop bein' so dramatic. *That's* what you need to do."

He got up and walked down the stairs, still shaking his head and mumbling under his breath, "Geez…"

I listened to the growl of the diesel engine as he started his truck and left. I stared at the impression on the bed from where he'd been sitting, hugging the comforter up to my neck, hearing him mumble,

"Geez…" over and over. My desperation boiled over until I was absolutely furious.

"I gotta get the fuck outta here."

The next day, shoving clothes in my bag and gathering stacks of CDs, Beth helped me get packed. I was flying to Pennsylvania to stay with my mom, get my GED, and get the hell outta dodge.

Dad barked up the stairs to hurry up, he needed to be back in town by five, and was getting angrier by the minute that he had to drive me to the airport. Beth, in complete Beth fashion, grabbed the nearest article of clothing she could get her hands on, and chucked it down the stairs right at his face, "She's gettin. Fuckin'. *Ready*!"

"That's what friends are foooor…." Dionne Warwick

I always thought visiting my mom and leaving home would hit the reset button. That I'd feel better once I was with someone who understood I was wrestling with depression, not trying to be a burden to everyone. But inevitably I'd remember, somewhere between the first hug and the car ride up the mountain, that she only ever made me feel worse. I was just trading out one evil for another.

In hindsight I realized I often made it to her house to be bedridden with what felt like the flu for two days. A sudden onset of chills and exhaustion would hit me, and she'd go into Dr. Kevorkian mode. Warming up tomato soup and recounting every horrible story about her past and my father she could muster.

"Rebecca your daddy's not capable of loving anyone, he cheated on me for *years,* but I just didn't wanna tell you girls. All he cares about is his job and his money. Rebecca he couldn't care less about you girls and me."

I was always too tired to argue or really question what she said. Both my parents had told me awful things about one another my entire life, always set out to prove once and for all that the *other* one never really loved us. That they themselves had put up with years of abuse to try and save my sister and me.

"Your daddy never wanted to come home, he didn't give a damn about you girls! It was *me* who begged him to take us on vacations, to spend time with us."

"*You'll* see. I've known who your mother *really* is my whole life, but I just didn't wanna cause a fuss Rebecca. I mean the things I could tell you... you wouldn't even believe. That woman is sick."

But I *did* believe.

Every time.

That was the problem.

No matter how much I knew my parents lied, something in me still clung to their stories for solid ground. When you're in a low place, you tend to not question negative things, because they just make your environment make that much more sense. So no matter how outlandish the story, they sneak past reasoning without much hesitation.

What you tell children, they will believe, and continue to believe in honest faith. And I was most definitely still a child.

It was my second night there, and I took my usual walk down to the creek, the thick snow crunched under my feet. I felt nervous out there by myself at night, not like back at home. The snow insulated everything making my steps echo against the dark cold. I remember seeing huge paw prints and wondering how fresh they were. It wasn't strange to see large black bears in that area waddle down the mountain side for a drink. I plopped down in the snow, clearing away a small space with my boots. The moon sparkled off the surface of the creek, it was motionless, winding through the tree line like a slab of obsidian. I lit my cigarette reverently, the spark reminding me I was still in the real world.

I propped my elbows on my knees, the snow slowly cooling the back of my legs. The creek was hypnotizing in the moonlight, you could hardly tell where the water line began it was so still, I thought about how cold it must be.

If I leaned forward a little more, I'd roll and sink right to the bottom, with the frigid temperature, it'd probably shock me enough I wouldn't fight all that much, and my boots'd drag me down anyways. Then my mom wouldn't have to find me. It'd be some neighbors downstream. That'd be the best way. Rather than taking her pills, this'd take away anyone's guilt in it being *their* meds. I wouldn't traumatize anyone by it being in their house.

Leaning forward slowly, further and further, staring into the black, my boot popped out from under me, dunking into the icy water with a startling splash! I jolted, jumping to my feet as embers from my cigarette flew into the air and sparkled to the ground.

"What the FUCK am I doing!?" It was as if I'd snapped out of a trance, as if someone had been lulling me to sleep. I shoved my hands in my pockets and marched back toward the house. "I gotta call Vern," I thought, "What the fuck am I doin'…"

My sopping boot squished up the stairs 'n I grabbed the cordless phone on the way to the guest room. I dialed her cellphone number as I shut the door behind me, starting to cry and wishing my friend was with me. It rang and rang and rang as I paced the floor.

"DUDE. PLEASE pick up the phone"

Voicemail.

Voicemail again.

I gave it a minute. Removed my boots and put on dry socks, then tried again. But this time it rang once, and went straight to voicemail.

Ok what the hell Vern.

I called again.

Straight to voicemail.

Now I was getting worried about *her*. This wasn't like her.

Then the phone rang on my end.

"Vern!"

"It's Beth. Dude. The fuckin' house just got busted. Veronica's in handcuffs, they busted in with shotguns. Everyone's goin' to jail 'n the guys are gettin' deported!"

"What."

I could hear Beth puffing her cigarette and pacing frantically.

"Oh my God, oh my God Becc…. They busted in the place with fuckin' shot guns and vests on, screaming in Spanish to put their hands up. I'm about to go sneak in and grab some stuff outta the house before they seal the place up."

"I'm so confused. Wait, so. Vern's in jail!? Like right now!? How did you find out?"

"I was ridin' by the house dude. They were pullin' laundry baskets of coke out from under the fuckin' house dude! We had NO idea what they were runnin' outta that place, no fuckin' clue. Holy shit Becc, holy fuckin' shit… I'm freakin' out."

"Beth…. Oh my…. I was tryin' to call Vern's cell but she didn't answer-"

"Yeah I'll tell ya why! I bet you fuckin ANYthing, fuckin' Johnny had it in his back pocket. I guarantee. I bet it was buzzin' while they were readin' her her rights so he turned it off. Becca they already knew the guys names and personal information. Like, they've been watchin' em for *years*."

In that moment, this tiny little voice inside me said, "Now aren't you glad *you* weren't there? What are the odds that you just happened to get outta town 48 hours before this happened? You *know,* without a doubt, you woulda been sitting right next to Veronica if your dad hadn't made you angry enough to leave. Funny how things work like that huh…"

I couldn't wrap my head around how long the house had evidently been under surveillance. There'd been a champagne color Buick Le Sabre that stayed parked across the street some days, in the parking lot of a closed real estate office. I'd gotten a weird feeling about it a few times but not enough to mention anything. Was that the cops? Oh my gosh…there were pictures of me *all over* that house. I mean it was one birthday party, holiday bash, and weekend binge after another, documented and stuck to their fridge with magnets and scotch tape. Guess who's never runnin' for political office…

Fuck.

And here's Vern, takin' the heat like she was the only one there.

I'd been making stupid decisions, acting completely powerless, and tempting fate loooooong before I sat and stared into that creek. I'd been pushing the edge, sassing God just to see if something would finally break loose and send me into another direction, anywhere but here.

Now we knew why the guys had NO chill about our maniacal laughter at my terrible Anne Frank joke that night.

Sorry bout it.

But, lemme get this straight- not only have my incessant giggles gotten me reprimanded in church, in the house of the Lord, but *also,* surrounded by coke trafficking felons in a dilapidated drug house.

Is nowhere safe?

Let me be *me*

CHAPTER SEVEN

"Son's gonna rise in a mile, in a mile
you'll be feelin' fine."

Son's Gonna Rise

Citizen Cope

The GED class in downtown Bethlehem was a motley crew, and *exactly* where my lil scared straight butt needed to be. Here I sat, amidst recovering meth addicts, struggling single moms, and sometimes homeless adults trying to start over. This was *not* where I saw myself ending up in the sixth grade, flaunting my Roxy watch and new platform flip flops. Not at *all*. Stupid Honorable Mention ribbon…. I'll show y'all!

I became quick friends with a guy in class we all lovingly nicknamed Theo. He always sported a different Cosby sweater for the day, proudly showing it off as he entered. Our teacher, Glenda, often brought him in, finding him on sidewalks in the early morning; sleeping off a long night or beat up. It was apparent his mental state was caused not only from drugs, but also years of abuse. We all had a soft spot for Theo. He kept a stack of CDs with him and his Disc-man tucked in his coat at all times. He couldn't be without his music. We had that in common.

It was about a week into classes when Glenda called me up to her desk after I'd handed in an assignment.

"Rebecca you did great. Again. If you don't mind me asking, *why* are you here?"

I thought about it really hard. I knew I was smart, but, I just never tried or cared to. Honestly, I guess I'm here, because of me.

"I guess, I dunno. I just, never liked school 'n, had other things goin' on I guess? Just lazy." I shrugged.

"Well, here's the thing," she said, "if you'll help me tutor and get your hours in, when you take your test and get a high score, which I know you will, you'll get to receive your high school diploma as opposed to a GED. How's that sound?"

96

"Sure! Sounds good to me!"

Bless you Glenda. I so badly needed someone to have a little faith in me, and to give me a little responsibility. She and I would go out for lunches and girl talk a few times before classes were over. It felt so good to have someone I looked up to not only hear me, but *wanna* hear what I had to say.

The door started to crack open on my depression. I was feeling like I could actually be of service and make a contribution. Like I wasn't just a burden.

During the weekends, I was working at a vintage dress shop with my mother, sorting and categorizing these extravagant gowns and coats. It was all packed in the downstairs of an old peach and lavender Victorian home, rows and rows of plastic wrapped dresses. You had to squeeze and swish your way through the aisles to go grab another stack.

It had been a little over a month since I'd last spoken to my father, since he dropped me off at the airport. Completely out of context one afternoon, mom stopped what she was doing and said, "You should call your dad and touch base with him, see how everything's goin'."

It wasn't like her to push me toward him, or worry about he and I's communication, but before I could say no, she was handing me her Motorola, "Here ya go. Just let him know how you're doin'."

"He probably won't even answer," I thought, but he did.

She stopped what she was doing and rested her chin in her hands to listen.

"Hey Dad."

"Well hey. How are ya?"

"Uhh I'm ok. Started GED classes."

"Oh yeah? Well, that's good."

"Yeah. The weather's startin' to get warmer up here too… so that's nice…"

"Alright."

Riveting conversation.

I scanned my brain for a common topic to get more than a monosyllabic answer from him.

"Oh yeah, I think Nathaniel's engagement shower was a couple weekends ago, did y'all go?"

"Nope, no we didn't make it, but uh, *I* did that."

"Did what?"

"Got married."

And then I set that whole gahdamn basement of priceless gowns on <u>FIRE</u>.

No, no I didn't. I did not commit arson that day, but that is *exactly* what I felt like doing. I don't remember at all what I said to him, or if I just snapped the phone shut as my knees buckled, but I do remember burying my face in the rack in front of me, sobbing into these thousand dollar dresses. (Thank God for that plastic wrap.)

My mom was ready to hand me a pack of Lexa-Pro, unbothered and completely composed. Already walking around the corner to console me.

"Dad got MARRIED."

"Oh Rebecca… I'm so sorry we didn't tell you."

"*We*? You and who? Who knew!?"

"Well, the day he brought you to the airport, your cousin Angie drove by the house a little after five on her way home, and there was a judge outside in the front yard with your dad and Janice, and there were two other cars pulling up. She called your sister as soon as she got home."

"So *everyone* already knew. Except for me. Who's moving *back* there in a few months, and no one thought to say anything. I don't even know… I'm so over this shit Mom."

"Rebecca-"

"NO. Ya know what, I'm gonna go sit outside, so you can call Samantha, and y'all can ONCE AGAIN gossip about how psychotic and pitiful I am. Go ahead, here's your fuckin' phone."

I grabbed the car keys, pushed through the clothes, up the stairs, and out the door. I felt like I couldn't get air until my feet hit the sidewalk. I didn't wanna hear *one more fucking word.*

One more thing. One more piece of information for them to withhold from me until *they* saw fit to divulge it, until they felt like some entertainment, turning my world upside down once again. Shaking their heads at my unstable emotions and ignorance.

In my raging fury, I wrote a letter to my Grandma Sheryl, my dad's mother, and I mean I unLOADED. I needed someone, ANYONE, to talk some sense into him, and to see he was not at all who he portrayed himself to be. I told her *everything*, pleading she understand that it's all been lies the whole time.

Now, in hindsight… this letter was *not* the smartest idea, especially to her, a protective mother, but

I was in the midst of a psychological whirlpool and throwing lines out to anyone that could possibly make sense out of it all.

When you feel your fingerstips being pealed from the ledge of reality, you'll grab for anything to keep you from falling.

I think the worst part for many of us, is when the people we reach for in desperation, choose to step back and just watch us drop alongside the rest of em.

Months later, Grandma Sheryl would wrap her arm around me at church and whisper, "Rebecca we need to talk about that letter you sent me. There's some things you just don't understand like you *think* you do. A man needs a woman in the house." I loved her *so* much, but she didn't get it. It seemed no one did. I told her to just forget it, I'd overreacted.

That would be one of the last days I went to church.

That year I'd managed to graduate before my class back at home, get my driver's license on my eighteenth birthday, and started working again. That's usually how I do things, nothing, and then everything all at once. I came home but assured Dad that I'd gotten a job and would soon be outta he and Janice's hair, but he insisted this was my home too and he didn't want me stayin' anywhere else.

"You don't need to be payin' rent somewhere when you can live here and put your money away," he repeated. It made me so happy that he actually wanted me home, maybe this new marriage was gonna be good for him.

In the middle of our conversation, as I filled him in on my new job and test scores, a rabbit came bouncing around the corner, and began sniffing my feet. Mind you, my dad's never been big about pets in the house. So now, here was this rabbit, free roaming his white carpeted living room, kicking little turd pellets behind him like a sputtering exhaust pipe.

I was, in a word, delighted.

It seemed karma had hopped right up and presented itself before me, with a fluffy white tail and skid marks to boot.

"OH! Who's this," I squealed with devious excitement.

"That's Gerald," he sighed, rolling his eyes, "she likes rabbits."

I won't go into great detail, and yes, suddenly having a new stepmom is awkward for all of us, but I added a *whole other level* of crap on top of an already crappy situation. When all your friends are in on the latest Janice prank, ya know things have gotten a little out of hand.

Beth and I smoked a couple blunts, then feeling adventurous and displeased with the way the living room had been rearranged, we took it upon ourselves to move all the furniture around one afternoon.

At first it was completely harmless, just sliding the couches to other side of the room, but then after a couple weeks into the silent battles, Janice was coming home to find the couch on the front porch and the chairs in the kitchen. It was glorious, and *I,* was being an absolute twat.

Luckily years later I was able to formally apologize for bein' such a little asshole, and thank her for being there for our dad. In all honesty, it was never really her that was always making things extremely sneaky and uncomfortable, it had always been him.

It was just easier to be mad at her.

As soon as he'd announced their engagement, he became nauseatingly affectionate with her, always making a point of it being right in front of me, keeping me in conversation until I'd finally get uncomfortable and walk out of the room. He was talking to me in the kitchen one night, standing behind her with his chin on her shoulder, rubbing her stomach as he spoke to me. I was so disgusted I started shaking. I marched out to the front porch to call Beth and she was already on her way with a bowl packed. Disgusted doesn't even begin to cover it. I wanted to peel my skin off.

He was always reminding me I couldn't just knock on the bedroom door and ask about transmission fluid or belt squeals anymore, things were different now No matter *how much* I assured him, "I. GET IT." he'd continue to go in depth, making sure I *knew* it was because they were having sex. So *again*, just in case I missed it, I can't just come knocking on the door at any time.

I wanted to vomit.

I reminded him I could just find somewhere else to stay, I could crash at a friends for a while. I was eighteen and making minimum wage, but I could figure something out, but he always insisted I stay, and I always felt somehow responsible for him, for looking out for him.

I kicked and screamed about coming home, but I was also trying to prove him wrong, to show him *I'd* never leave him, no matter what. I'd be the one person in the family who stayed by his side, and I knew eventually he'd see that and stop treating me like the enemy. *Then* I'd truly be able to move on, knowing the wounds were mended and he knew how sorry I was for ever helping Mom hurt him.

How many times do we put our lives on hold, awaiting the end of tasks we know we'll never finish? Outlandish unrealistic goals we know we'll never reach? How many days have I put off writing this book until every inch of our apartment is completely spotless?

Scrubbing the kitchen countertops until it's time to feed the dog, make dinner, and fold the laundry. I dunno if that addiction of progressive procrastination ever really goes away, maybe we just have to get better at callin' bullshit on ourselves.

Either way, I was *not* ready at that time to admit I was imprisoning myself, suscepting myself to the very environment I was sickened by.

I wasn't at all ready to see what that kinda self-analysis really uncovered.

Carolyn, our boss and part owner at the coffee house I'd started working at, had a knack for hiring people who needed a safe haven and a fresh start. The place was a bit of a rehabilitation center for a lot of us, and working there brought me back to life. I was extremely happy again. Just like Glenda, she'd had enough faith in me, for me to have just enough in myself.

I adored the girls I worked with, sliding back and forth barefoot through melted ice cream and coffee grounds. The line stayed out the door and down the the side ramp during the summers. We'd dance around each other calling out lattes and milkshakes while our regular local customers cracked jokes 'n stopped by for cigarettes and chit chats. We had a ball.

I even started singing off 'n on with my friend TJ's band (who I was secretly madly in love with, but we'll get to that later.) I started trusting the good nature in people again and not being afraid to be seen. And later on, when depression started pressing down on me again, Carolyn was there. She drove to the house and snuck a note in my car after I'd called outta work. I didn't know what to tell her. I was too embarrassed to go in and face everyone with red and swollen eyes. My life was fine, there was no reason for me to be struggling like this except by my own self-loathing, and I was furious with myself for that. No one saw me like that except for Beth and Vern, and I'd still done by best to hide it from them.

I'd gone so long without the awful chills down my spine walking through the house, or the noises

106

waking me up, but then it started happening again. It felt like there was this peach pit inside of me just rotting under the surface, as if these nightly visitors had to pop up to remind me who I really was, that nothing had actually changed.

There was a night I slept on the couch downstairs after my sister's dog Buddy had died. I heard his nails tick against the wood floor as he pranced toward the living room. I tucked my neck into the cushions, knowing how he loved to slide his cold snout under your head to wake you. I felt his wet nose brush my hair as he excitedly sniffed behind my ear, "Buddy booooy lemme sleeeeeep." I begged, then quickly sat up in disbelief, remembering he hadn't been alive, not to mention in that house for at least two years. I could still feel his cold wet nose on my scalp.

I shared these stories with friends who delighted in them, squealing how fun it was that I experienced these things, but *I* didn't always see it that way. Not when I'd been told my entire life I was unstable and delusional. It just made me question my sanity even more. I'd always talked to my angels and had lots of protection and uncanny insight, but why couldn't I just fucking get my shit together! Everything would be fine 'n then boom! Back in the pit again. Why do I keep doin this to myself!?

I had this repeating nightmare of being trapped at the bottom of a silo or water tank. The walls were filthy white tiles discolored from years of stagnant water pooling at the bottom of the clogged drain. I was always either stuck at the bottom, or staring into it from the top, as if I knew I was damned to fall back down there again. Dripping water echoed against the ceramic. The place had been abandoned for years. I felt like it must've been an old swimming pool at a mental hospital or something. The sickening smell of urine and chlorine still hung in the air. Over and over, I'd end up there once again, my neck arched back as I looked up at the ladder far beyond my reach. The slick slimy walls went up for what seemed like three stories. There was no way I was gettin' out.

They'd moved on and forgotten about me.

It's crazy to pinpoint these bouts of darkness in a timeline, because alongside these awful images I recollect, that still feel yucky to this day, I was also having some of the best days of my life. Having an absolute blast, goin' to shows, fishin' trips, road trips, jam sessions, late night talks and bonfires, I was *so* happy. At the time I didn't see the irony in how these two sides of me could not take turns, but live alongside one another simultaneously. Acknowledging each existed just as much as the other.

I understood bipolar, mania, schizophrenia, all that mess from years of therapy. I was pretty good at bein' a hypochondriac in every way and going through checklists on my mental health daily, but *this* wasn't that. It also didn't quite have the shelf life or the melancholy that depression did, it was different.

This had been around since I was a child, since I could remember, evolving as I aged. This felt like an ominous tone in the background of a symphony that suddenly became deafening if it got too quiet.

But most days, it was barely noticeable. Unlike a feeling of paranoia, it was more like a brand or an echo, like an alarm going off I knew I didn't set. As long as I stayed distracted, I started to believe I may never hear from it again.

By this point, although I had plenty of guy friends, I'd never *actually* dated anyone, and only ever kissed a few boys. I never thought of myself as insecure, I mean I thought I was attractive, just not enough for anyone I liked to actually be interested in me. I felt like my lack of experience *and* boobs kinda put me in the dugout.

109

You could read it on my face, "I have no idea how this works, and what do I do with my hands?"

My first kiss was in a hotel room I'd snuck out to with a boy I'd met at a Mormon youth function. Kinda overshot the first kiss gettin' a hotel room 'n sharin' a bed 'n all, but, there it is. Naturally, the place was a rat's nest and had tropical lights hanging on the reception desk. The only place on the beach that would rent rooms to an eighteen year old. We sat up drinking warm Budweiser and playing cards with his friend who was leaving to go on his mission the following month. I was smitten. I had a huge thing for Seth Green at the time 'n this boy stood at just about the same height. I remember the phone to our room rang the next morning and I went into hysterics screaming, "DON'T PICK IT UP!" I just *knew* it was my parents, they'd somehow found out where I was, and were calling to say, "Whore." and then hang up, never to speak to me again. I was sixteen I think? Sixteen 'n gettin' my first kiss in a hotel room with Kelly Clarkson singin' Miss Independent on MTV in the background. Sounds about right.

And so it went on from there. Sloppily trying to form romantic relationships, but so absolutely terrified to even show the slightest inkling of interest, I usually just settled for beers and smokin' pot with em instead. All my friends were on their third and fourth boyfriends, and I could barely hold someone's hand without shaking profusely.

"Maybe I'm *not* fucked up...what if I'm just gay 'n I don't know it!?" I lined up the mental checklist, and began the assessment. "I mean, it *would* answer why I've never actually dated, and why I become paralyzed around guys I have a crush on..."

But then I realized the latter statement kinda put the former in question already. Then I had to acknowledge that even the thought of being physical with another girl, made my nose wrinkle. Like when those guys I didn't like tried to put their arm around me at church dances. God sees you creeper!

Well *that* was a short lived experiment, but, an honorable attempt nonetheless.

Great so, we're back at square one then.

It's just *me*. I'm just fucked up.

Neato.

Remember TJ? The friend I told you I was madly in love with but absolutely positively could not let him know that? Well, eventually I let him know that. A long eventually. It was pretty much forced. We'd met when I was still in middle school and been friends ever

111

since. He was constantly dating someone, or sleeping with someone, or talking about how he *wanted* to sleep with someone. That intimidated the daylights outta my Josie Grosie self, so I settled for bein' the friend he called every night after he dropped his girlfriend off by her curfew.

I didn't have a curfew. *I* was a grown woman who did whatever the fuck she wanted. (Except for openly express my emotions and sexuality. There's *that*.)

We'd sit around a bonfire 'n drink beers til the sun came up almost every night. I'd leave once I heard the garbage trucks making their rounds, then I'd go home and pray he'd realize he was madly in love with me, breakup with his girlfriend and then it'd just be eternal bliss.

I'd listen to Billy Joel's, *She's Got A Way*, and my heart would ache thinking, "One day, *someone* will think about me like that. It'll happen… eventually."and then eventually, it did. Not the song yet, but I lost my virginity. (Who came up with that terminology anyway? Lost it. As if a strong wind took it.)

He and his girlfriend broke up, and after multiple bonfires and ridiculous amounts of growing sexual tension, I finally gave in and admitted yes, although I'd kept myself fully clothed in cardigans and wool socks lying in bed next to him many a night, I *was,* in fact, extremely attracted to him. I just hadn't the slightest idea how I was supposed to relay that message without actually saying the words.

And I was *never* going to say those words.

I had no idea how I was supposed to act as a girlfriend, and I never actually called him my boyfriend. I was too terrified he'd correct me and say we were just talking and I'd look like a complete fool, so I just said nothing. I followed his lead and tried to act comfortable, but I was so *not* comfortable.

My body had gone completely numb the first night we slept together. This had not even slightly happened to me during make-out sessions, and I mean I felt <u>nothing</u>. I went numb from the neck down and then could barely remember it afterwards. I was afraid I wouldn't be able to get up off the bed I was so shaky.

He sat there playing guitar and asked me wasn't I gonna call anyone.
"What, like, for a *ride?*"

I don't think that's what he meant.

I was so lost. I didn't know what I was supposed to do, or who I was supposed to call, or what color ribbon I was supposed to pin to my shirt to let everyone know. I was too busy wigging out silently.

Is that what happens to *everyone* their first time?

Did I have a stroke or something?

I feel like I wasn't even there, like I left as soon as it started.

All my limbs feel like white noise, why do all my limbs feel like white noise?

I'm lightheaded.

What the fuck is wrong with me?

Am I in *shock!*? Oh my God, am I in shock *just* from having *sex*!? Oh great, I really *am* fucked...

It didn't take too long before I pulled the plug. The more I told myself to relax, trust him, be vulnerable. I. Could. Not. I wanted so badly to just be close to him and enjoy the fact that I'd finally gotten what I wanted, I was dating my best friend, how could it not be more perfect!? But everything in me screamed I was in imminent danger, and he couldn't be trusted.

I broke up with him in a letter, I wanted to make sure he had the words written down explaining how wonderful he really was, but I just couldn't do it. Maybe we'd mature and try again a few years down the road, but for right now I just can't. Besides, we were moving into a townhouse together with a mutual friend in a few months, I figured it best we go ahead 'n get through the break up *now,* and get the water under the bridge before we were sharing a bathroom and what not. Simple. Clean break. Done and done. Now we could live together without any tension. Mmhm…

You can probably guess how smooth that went.

Diabolical.

CHAPTER EIGHT

"Ya just keep on usin' me, until ya use
me up."

Use Me

Bill Withers

I'd gotten almost a twenty four hour head start
on moving in before TJ and our buddy Marshall got to
the house to move the rest of their stuff in. They knew
how much I cherished my alone time, I needed to burn
my sage and get my space set up. It was around 10:30
in the mornin' and I was happily sippin' coffee and
moving trash bags from my little two door Saturn to my
new room upstairs. Excited and nervous, I'd never lived
in any kind of apartment complex before and this was a

new town where I'd need to find a new job and new bars that let me drink under 21.

Not long after I lugged the last trash bag inside, I heard a loud thump against the side of the townhouse. The sound had a hollow vibration to it, like you might hear from a kickball on the playground. I assumed it was just some kids in the complex goofin' off. But it kept on. It shook the walls of the house every few thumps. I looked out the windows, checking the perimeter for anybody in the parking lot, but everyone was at the pool.

"Ohhhh, I bet it's our neighbor's kid throwin' a ball against our adjoining patio fence…" I thought. That'd make sense.

And then it was two o-clock, then five, then seven, and then it was getting dark and the noise still hadn't stopped.

"That is one bored child," I thought, "Aren't they gonna let the kid inside for dinner? Unless… *Unless* it's those pooka shell necklace frat boy fuckers that cat called me earlier! I'll kill em!"

I looked out the windows again, looking completely paranoid, but everyone was inside for the night. By nine, when it still hadn't stopped, I was gettin' pretty freaked out. What the hell could possibly be hittin' the side of the house hard enough to feel it in the floors?

I decided to call my friend JoJo in Tampa, she'd calm me down with her Shakespeare monologues and Jim Morrison trivia.

"Becc!"

"Ay girl!!"

"Girl what are you doin? I was just thinkin' boutcha!" I heard her lighter spark as she got comfortable.

I didn't let her know just yet that I was pacing the downstairs with my Louisville Slugger.

"Just, ya know, gettin' moved in and situated before the boys get here. Marshall should be pullin' up in an hour or so."

We talked about who knows what for a few more minutes until I finally interrupted.

"Girl, I'm so sorry, lemme tell you why I *really* called. Ok, so there's been this banging noise against the house that seriously started around lunch time, and *has not stopped* since. Like I dunno if somebody's fuckin' with me or what, but like, it's gettin' late and it's <u>not</u> stopping."

"Whaaaat!?" She puffed and exhaled with a squeak, "Uh yeah girl, I'd be a lil freaked too. Do you know anybody around there yet?"

"Not really dude, I literally just go there today. Sam's somewhat close, but I say that as in like a forty five minute drive."

"Hmmm… 'n you've thoroughly inspected the perimeter?" When she gets invested, she starts soundin' a lil like Johnny Depp in *Fear and Loathing*.

"Yep! Nobody. Everyone's inside from the pool 'n its quiet otherwise."

"Mmmmm, I mean I dunno Becc. That sounds like some ghosty mess to *me*. I know you ain't a stranger to no spirits," she laughed, "Do you by any chance know who lived there before?" She herself came from a long line of gypsies, and we were constantly giving one another readings. Her with her cards 'n me lookin up into the ethers. She was always teaching me yiddish phrases 'n old family superstitions, 'n I'd just quote back lines from *Funny Girl*.

I walked into the kitchen, squinting at the French doors that opened to the back patio. It was now completely dark outside so I could only see my own reflection, but it *felt* like someone was looking back at me through the glass. I wanted to turn on the patio

120

lights, to catch whoever was out there, but my gut said, "Mmmm, maybe ya *don't* wanna do that."

"What? Oh! Um, oh oh oh yeah, I'm not really positive who lived here before us. I think some woman alone in her fifties maybe? Hold on Marshall just texted. Ok sweet, he'll be here soon! Can you seriously just talk to me about anything and distract me until he gets here?"

"You got it girl."

I sat on the couch in the living room, tapping my foot against the coffee table and biting my lips. I remember her telling me something about her brother, and then I interrupted her again,

"I am so sorry dude, I'm tryin' to pay attention but that is the SEVENTH time the thump has happened since you started talkin'. I'm freakin' the fuck out JoJo, it sounds like its hitting against the patio doors."

"Girl do you for real feel like it's a bad spirit?"

"I don't know, I feel so crazy like, assuming that's the logical explanation, but even so, being raised in my religion-"

WHAM! The French doors rattled from the heavy blow!

My knees came to my chest and my butt left the couch cushions as I screamed!

121

"WHAT THE FUCK BECC! ARE YOU OK!?"

"JO! CAN YOU HEAR THAT!?"

"Yes. What the fuck Rebecca. Oh my Gooooooood I don't feel good about thiiiiiis…. That happened right as you were gonna talk about religion…"

Now it was slamming the doors harder and harder, Jo was keeping count on the other end of the phone, asking me how far away Marshall was now. I was holding onto my knees, curled up and shaking. There was no way this wasn't actually happening now, Jo could hear it too. Finally I heard a different thumping sound, it was the techno base bumping from Marshall's car!

"JO, MARSHALL'S HERE! I'LL CALL YOU BACK!"

I hung up the phone, busted through the front door and was standing barefoot in his headlights before he could even get the car in park.

"BeBe… are you ok?"

My face was white as a ghost, and since I'm the one that everyone else usually runs to when they're scared, he already knew somethin' was most definitely *not* ok.

"I need you to come inside with me, right now!"

I took his hand and furiously ran him into the house like a mouse leading a circus bear. He stands a good foot taller and has about 200 pounds on me.

"LISTEN! There's been this bumping noise against the house all day. ALL. DAY. And so I called Jo to keep me company til you got here, but it just kept on more and more, and then right when I was about to bring up religion it went BAM against those doors!!!"

Pointing at the patio doors in front of us, I felt safe enough now to walk over and hit the switch for the outdoor lights, but to my surprise, nothing had been moved. The lock on the gate was still locked and not a single cigarette butt was outta place.

We both slowly walked out onto the stoop, looking around the small area for anything funny, and then BAM! He gasped and whipped his head to lock eyes with me as his mouth dropped open.

"There it is! See! You heard it too!"

We both stepped back, looking up at the brick exterior of the house in unison, as if we might catch someone clung to the side like Spiderman.

"Uhh…ok I *definitely* heard that… I don't understand where that could be coming from. It hit, the side." He was just as confused as I was.

We walked back through the doors and into the kitchen, shutting the doors gently behind us. We took two steps and then there it was again, except this time it was louder from *inside* the house.

Now Marshall was going pale.

We turned to one another and held hands, without saying a word our eyes quietly said, "This might be it. This is how we die booboo. Should we turn on Madonna and make a Tom Collins for the road?"

We chain smoked for an hour or so to calm ourselves down, he started looking for a logical explanation of why the noise would be louder from inside the house as opposed to out.

"OH! Bebe, I know what it is. I bet it's these speakers, they're plugged into the subwoofer, 'n I bet it's just shortin' out or something and thumping against the doors."

I looked at these tiny little speakers he had propped on top of the trim work at the left and right corners. He fumbled with the wiring and they made a meek little crackling noise, but that was about it. He unplugged them assuring me that'd fix it.

"Yeah… I bet that's it."

That, was *not* it. He knew it wasn't either, but I appreciate the attempt.

We both laid in our beds that night waiting to hear it again until we finally passed out.

When I came downstairs the next morning, my feet had barely hit the linoleum in the kitchen when a heavy thud hit the patio doors. I sighed, grabbed the coffee out of the cabinet, and filled the pot with water.

So this is happenin' huh, we're doin' this.

Marshall came down the stairs not long after, and as soon as he came around the corner, there it was again. His feet left the floor as he shrieked and grabbed at his boxers to save himself.

"BeBe what the hell!?"

"Yeah so... *not* the speakers bud," I poured him a cup of coffee 'n grabbed two cigarettes, "All I'm sayin is, he better not fuck with my alarm clock, that's all I ask."

I have a talent for adapting to extremely uncomfortable situations. It *should have* cued me in right there, how ridiculously low my standards were if my *only* request for a demented door banger, was that it not mess with my alarm clock. I mean honestly...

Things only continued to progress over the next few months.

Objects were constantly moved around. I'd wake up to my blinds carefully pulled down and closed

125

over the shells and stones on my window sill. Friends would get creeped out in the shower, hearing children giggling and feeling like someone's hand was on their shoulder.

My buddy Meredith stood up from the kitchen table one evening, freaking out after asking me to repeat what I'd whispered in her ear, but then realizing I was standing across the room at the oven.

All the while, TJ experienced *nothing*. No matter how many people walked out of our bathroom wide eyed and vowing to never pee alone again, he didn't believe a word of it.

"You guys are fuckin' nuts." he kept sayin'. He even stood on the patio throwing a ball against the house one afternoon mocking us, "Uh oh guuuuuys!!! It's the creepy scary monster dude!"

Marshall and I stared at him in terror. NOT amused.

"DO NOT. DO THAT," we warned him sternly, "Do not make fun of him. STOP IT."

Jo was in town, and that night she and Meredith stayed over, and we piled onto my tiny bed, Googling, "Signs your house is haunted. SEARCH." My witchy girls and I were gonna get down to the bottom of this.

126

I'd cleaned and vacuumed my room that morning, getting guest nests ready for the girls and desperately lookin' for the paperwork with my new pin number. I'd shoved it into my purse the last time I'd walked over to the ATM, and now I was terrified somebody'd found it and would proceed to wipe out every cent of my 64 dollar fortune.

We were about twelve paranormal lists deep when I told the girls I had to pee, "Don't read anymore 'til I get back!"

Before even shutting the bathroom door behind me, I pulled the shower curtain to the side (as one does) to make sure nobody was creeping, and heard TJ growling loudly in my right ear!

I jumped, bout peein' myself, and threw my elbow behind me to knock him in the ribs for bein' a dick!

But there was no one there. I stuck my head outta the bathroom to catch him, but his bedroom door was still shut.

"Y'AAAAAAAALL!!!!!!!!"

I ran and jumped on the bed between them, rockin' myself back and forth,

"Please tell me one of y'all just tried to scare me and growled in my ear…"

127

Their lips slowly curled downward, shaking their heads no in unison. Now they were as scared as I was.

"That is enough. Thaaaaat is enough."

"Becc what the fuck happened!?"

"Y'all… not only did someone growl in my ear when I was FUCKING CHECKING FOR SERIAL KILLERS BEHIND THE SHOWER CURTAIN…it was legit like, TJ's VOICE. Like I was throwin' bows 'n about to chase him back to his room. I just… Uh uh. No ma'am. Nooooo ma'am!"

They shut the laptop and we all high pitch girl screamed for about 30 seconds. I still had to pee, but I wasn't goin' alone this time, so they agreed to stand posted outside the door.

My foot touched the carpet as I went to stand up from my bed, and *there* was the paper work with my pin number. Neatly folded, and placed in front of my night stand without a crease on it.

"OHHHHH NO. NOOOOO NO NO NO NO NO MA'AM. MMM- MMMMMMMM NO MA'AM!!!"

I tucked that foot right back under my butt, digging my nails into the girls arms,

"NOPE! Y'all are sleepin' right here with ME!"

I saged the fuck outta that house. I saged that house til our neighbor's smoke alarms coulda gone off. That was *enough,* I had had it. Nope nope nope. I reached my breakin' point, it took a while, but I put my foot down on the spooky shit.

Now *here's* the pattern I didn't really wanna recognize at the time.

How often was I letting people push my buttons and cross boundaries before I spoke up or even tried to defend myself? How often did I just put up with being taunted and isolated, because someone told me I was just nuts? How often were lies and sadistic motives right in front of my face, but I managed to reason them away every time. "It's not like that *all* the time," I'd say, "It's only every once in a while. That's not who they *are.* They wouldn't *purposefully* try to make me feel bad."

Now, not all of us have these freaky deaky experiences, but I believe we all have our different languages of perception, and so things will be translated for us specifically in ways that will impact us most. That will get our attention and we'll hear loud and clear, and for me, that's through the unseen.

I'd become *way* too good at forgiving pathological lying and complete fabrications of reality.

I grew up listening to my parents, and thinking, "Ok *that's* not what happened, but you seem pretty adamant about your version of the story though so I'll allow it…"

With time, that kinda constant forgiveness and overlooking of dishonesty, becomes second nature. Everything is forgiven. No matter how cruel, or how awful someone may act, our reaction is to see them as a child, they know not what they do. How could we be so cruel as to force them to accept responsibility when they had *no idea* they were hurting anyone? We need to be nice and forgive right?

So we let em keep on doin what they do. Lettin' assholes manipulate us, and paranormal jerks scare us into a UTI. It's as if we've decided since *obviously* they'll never be taking responsibility for their own actions, the only option left is for *us* to pick it up and fix it. We begin loading ourselves down with someone else's traits, analyzing them over and over until we don't remember which ones aren't our own anymore.

Things were *not* good at the house, not at all. TJ ended up moving out not long after he and Marshall had gotten into a heated argument one night. I was listening to them going back 'n forth as I brushed my teeth, and then hearing it escalate, I ran out of the bathroom, pinning TJ against the banister to separate them. I packed my bag that night and drove up to Pennsylvania a few weeks later, getting a job at a coffee shop downtown 'til I could sort things out.

I was constantly packin' up that green army bag, throwin' it in the back seat and leaving in the middle of the night. I didn't *feel* like I was running from anything. I was just nomadic, free spirited. I just, liked to drive at night and smoke with the radio on, why not drive twelve hours up I-95?

I'd been up there for about a week when I got a voicemail from TJ late one night. I could hear Billy Joel in the background. He was driving and listening to *She's Got A Way*, "I just needed to call you," he sniffled, "I'm listenin' to this song 'n it just makes me think about you. I love you Becc."

That was *not* how I'd imagined that song playin out.

I'd never even told him about listening to that song, and this, this does me no good. *Now* he calls about it? Now? It's too late, I've already ruined it. I'd pushed him away just like I did everyone else. What the fuck is *wrong* with me?

I don't know that I even had the guts to call him back. I think I'd already fallen into another self-loathing cycle, I didn't wanna bother him, I'd already made enough of a mess. He needed to move on and stick with the girl he had. One that didn't feel the need to pack up 'n relocate every six months.

Frankly, I'm a little embarrassed to say, that I was running *so* much, and was so insanely flakey during these years, I cannot even get the timeline straight.

How I found myself working at the old coffee house at home again or how I managed to move multiple times again before the age of twenty one. Obviously I had a lot of people pullin' me outta the fire, and again in hindsight, I can see I was battling a lot more inner turmoil than I thought.

I think trying to open up and be ok with the idea of someone loving me, had pulled the pin out of the grenade that was my psyche. I knew I definitely wasn't A-sexual, 'n I wasn't gay, 'n it wasn't that I didn't have guys that were interested in me, but for the *love of God*, I could *not* seem to stop running in an absolute panic! It was like the second there was that moment of, "Ok and now, relax into their arms," I had to get the <u>fuck</u> outta there.

I think we need people in our lives to pull those pins sometimes, and not even so much with conscious

132

intent, but simply by exposing us to their own perspective of the world, and how they see us in it. Just that in itself can be enough to shake our view of reality, if we can just listen. And whether she knew it at the time or not, I listened to everything Carolyn said to me, I took it all to heart and tucked it away in my chest.

She pulled me aside one day, and with her great Long Island accent she said to me,

"Ya know guhl, a lotta women aren't gonna like you at awl, cause you can talk to anyone, ya not tryin' to impress anyone. Not everyone's like that, ya know, can just *be* themselves. So don't take it personal."

I remember thinking it was random that she would say that, but I didn't realize at the time just *how much* she paid attention. That woman didn't miss a damn thing. If she saw somethin', good or bad, she had no problem pointin' it out. She walked up straight up to a new employee one mornin 'n quietly asked,

"When'd ya drop it?"

The rest of us poked our heads around the corner to listen, wondering why there was a sudden interrogation.

"What?" The girl responded nervously.

"Don't shit me guhl, I know ya on acid, ya can't be in here on that shit, go home."

133

And she did. She walked right out the back door and left.

"Wha? Carolyn. How the hell'd you know she was on acid? She *literally* just clocked in."

"I saw the way she watched that broom drop to the floor, she was watchin' the traces," she smiled and laughed, "Ya can't fool *me* honey."

She and another one of the owners, Franky, filled these tough but loving maternal roles that I needed *so* desperately at that time. I mean they busted us and called us out on so much shit, but always reminding us that it's just part of growin' up. Ya figure this shit out along the way and respect others enough to apologize when ya fuck up.

One night after catching me and another employee using the work's storage apartment to throw a party. Franky laughed and said, "Ya got caught kid, the trick is, ya *don't* get caught!" She was laughing hysterically at our panicked faces, "Now come over here 'n help me finish this picture collage for the Christmas decorations."

When I left that job to go to massage school, I wrote Carolyn a long letter, thanking her for giving me a family when I felt like I didn't have one. Ten years later, walking my husband in the place to surprise her, I saw that letter framed on the back wall surrounded by photos of all the girls.

Along with a mug (my only piece of dinnerware on *many* of my moves) that read, "A Gentle Hand. A Warm Heart. A Gypsy Spirit," Carolyn wrote me a note in the journal she'd bought me for my new upcoming chapter.

"Remember, friends are like buttons on an elevator, some will take you down, and some will take you up. Never lose insight. Just keep spreading your sunshine to the lives you intertwine with. You'll always be that planet Venus, with such brilliance and warmth people feel great in your presence…. Go out, enjoy life, let it happen. Where there is peace and meditation, there is neither anxiety nor doubt."

It's hard to keep people anonymous when I just wanna shout their praises from the rooftops, but Carolyn, you know who you are. You showed me the support, love, and faith that I'd always needed. You spark the light in more lives than you could possibly imagine. Thank you for coming from your heart every day, it's healing the world.

CHAPTER NINE

"Who gave you permission to rearrange
me? Certainly not me."

Certainly

Erykah Badu

*A*side from packs of Camel Lights and family
size boxes of Cheez-Its, up until that point, I felt like
I'd never actually finished anything I started. So when I
graduated from massage school, it was a huge deal for
me. I'd done it. I'd managed to make it through all the
kinesiology, anatomy, and physiology courses so I
could get to the good stuff, the stuff I actually
understood.

My years workin' at the coffeehouse had made
me realize that my true passion, was people. I fucking
loved <u>people</u>. I laid in bed thinking about how I'd

always wanted to do some kind of counseling work or fill some sort of companionship role. Maybe because I'd seen how rare it was to find therapists that *actually* are in it to listen and help, as opposed to imposing their opinions and superiority onto their clients. "I'd take everyone's problems home with me though... I'd be burnt out after one month," I thought, "But what about massage... I could comfort and help people, without having to talk. That might be better!" I got up outta bed, looked up massage schools in my state, and found one offering small intimate class settings, located in the middle of the mountains surrounded by creeks and horses.

Mmmmhm mmhm mmhm!

I ordered their brochure to be delivered so I could look it over, and got excited at the thought of enrolling at this gorgeous school. Carolyn was getting outta the business, and had actually mentioned to me, that I should think about it for myself. She saw what that place meant to me and how much I adored it, but I was only twenty years old and not sure if I wanted to do that forever. I pulled up in the driveway a few days later and thought, "If the brochure's in the mail, I'll go to massage school, but if it's *not*, I'm gonna talk to Dad about buyin' that coffeehouse."

Even though I know I ended up exactly where I need to be, I still dream about running another coffee house someday. I'll always miss being part of a safe place for people to check in and escape for a while. Coming down in their jammies from the upstairs apartments holding their empty mugs, leaving their jobs to vent for ten minutes, running in to share the great news that just happened to them. I can't get enough of it, it just doesn't get better than that. Practicing massage and bodywork taught me that I could make myself that safe space.

Even if it's just for thirty minutes, to be able to gift people a moment to unload, take some deep breaths, and be heard, it's wonderful. I thought the not talking part would make it completely different from counseling, but I hadn't realized just how many different ways we speak, and how many different ways we can be heard, and that words often don't have a hell of a lot to do with it.

We know when we're safe with someone, when we can put our bags down and take our shoes off. Our bodies start to release and soften, and our demeanor can change completely without any words spoken. I don't like to get too technical about reading energy off people or tuning in, because I think it can separate us from the fact it's just something we're *all* constantly doing whether we realize it or not. Whether we believe what we're picking up on or not. I think we all have our own ways of analyzing and understanding what it is we're sensing, whether it's a physical reaction, or words just falling out of our mouth before we even realize we're divulging intimate details to a total stranger.

I think it's kinda like, recognizing how a house plant leans toward the sunlight streaming through our window. Yes, we can study why and how they do that, and it's so cool, but all in all, it's just how living happens. How we naturally open and shine around people and environments that are nutrient dense and full of light, but close off and become weak when environments or people are devoid of such qualities. As living organisms, we instinctively reach for what brings us life, and close off from what brings us death, it's a natural thing right?

So, when I saw myself closing off, shaking profusely, and panicking in the middle of situations that I instinctively felt no threat was present, I had to ask myself, "Ok so… where exactly am I feeling like this may be pushing me toward sudden death? Why am I panicking, when I see no actual need to panic? Where am I having a total disconnect and opposing reactions in myself?"

I'd experienced trauma releasing from simple trigger point work during sessions, I saw how locked emotions were surfacing just from simple touch and being present, but I did *not* see where that was occurring in myself.

At all.

Again, I just thought I was fucked up for some reason, and eventually it would just... go away.

Eventually I'd stop shaking and clenching my jaw when the guy I was dating put him arms around me. Eventually I'd be able to let him touch me or hold me after we had sex. Maybe I'd even be able to sleep when I stayed the night, rather than stare at the ceiling in a cold sweat and change the license plate on my car at 6am with a butterknife from his kitchen.

But I didn't give eventually much of a chance.

I'd started seeing a friend, another friend I was secretly in love with, Jason. He was an incredible artist and fellow introvert who regularly hung out with the same group of misfits I did. I'd started working back at the beach as soon as my massage license came through, and I'd drive out once or twice a month to see him.

Sometimes it went well, and sometimes it didn't. I made sure there was enough space between us, and stayed busy enough, that if 'n when things didn't work out, it wouldn't be because I couldn't allow myself to be vulnerable with him.

It would simply be because we were just too busy.

It would be because I was just too independent and too much of a strong willed woman to wait around for some man to to make time for me. So I just made sure I gave minimal opportunities for said time, setting him up to fail constantly so I could respond, "Well, whatever, I had plans anyway. No a big deal. We're both busy."

Just as I'd always done with my dad.

Unfortunately, I think Jason and I were both too guarded to really trust anyone yet. We spent most of our visits projecting our biggest fears repeatedly, and simultaneously wishing we could move past them. Always having multiple conversations going on at once; what we said to one another, and what it was we really *wanted* to say. We'd decide to just go back to being friends, and then things seemed to change weeks later.

I was working ten and eleven hour days up the beach, doing massages back to back and putting money away for a new car and a place of my own. I hadn't moved in almost six months, I was gettin' antsy. I sat looking at job listings in Tahoe, California one night after work. I didn't even know anyone who'd ever *been* to Tahoe, but I'd always wanted to go. I mean it sounded nice!

"That'd be sweet," I thought, "it looks so pretty!"

A few days later, Shaunda, the esthetician that worked in the room next to mine, approached me in-between clients as we ran back and forth with hot laundry.

"Here's your sheets!! HEY! Before ya go, listen um, so, me and Thomas are movin' out to Truckee, California with my little boy when the season's over, but, we need a roommate and like, we don't know *anyone* out there... So like, I dunno if you'd even be interested, but it's *really* pretty, and it's like 15 minutes from Tahoe so, I dunno. I dunno if you'd be interested but-"

"WHAAAT!? Girl YES. For real."

"Really!? Oh my gosh! Ok! Well like, oh my gosh, ok. I'll text you this evening and we'll talk about dates and stuff!"

A couple months later, my dad and I were mapping out the route I'd drive to Truckee. It's kinda hard to get lost on I-40, but I didn't know if I wanted to go North at Albuquerque or drive up the coast. I was so excited I couldn't take it.

Dad and I had started getting along again, but he still wasn't taking my job seriously, so I did everything I could to prove to him that his hard work on me wasn't wasted. He constantly reminded me of the thousands of dollars he shelled out for me to go to school and that it had better be worth it. Then, not long after my license came through, one of my wisdom teeth became infected and my face was swelling. We had to make an emergency visit to an oral surgeon a couple hours away.

I remember him telling the surgeon, "Well let's just get all four taken out if we're already gonna be here." He snapped his billfold shut after sliding the signed receipt back to the receptionist and booking the appointment for the following week. Shaking his head at the total, he looked at me and said, "Welp, there ya go. There goes the down payment for your car."

I apologized the whole ride home. Deflated that I was just starting my career at twenty-one with a car about to break down, which meant I was already needing thousands of dollars before I even got a full paycheck. So when I put away seven thousand in tips after only a couple months of work, and walked up to him and said, "Is this enough for a down payment?"

It felt *really* good.

Money has always decided what side of the fence you're on with him, so I was ecstatic to be on the good side now. I wouldn't be a burden anymore. He wouldn't sigh heavily every time he saw me and roll his eyes in disgust.

I knew I needed a car big enough for me and Shaunda's full grown German Shepherd to sleep in the back with my massage table while we made our way to California. (I say "we" like me and the dog took turns driving. Although he *did* like to hop in the driver's seat when I went into gas stations.)

I worked nonstop that entire summer. Sometimes leaving Jason's house at five in the morning to make the three hour drive straight into work, get coffee brewin' for the gang, and do back to back massages until nine that night. I loved it.

I hadn't told Jason about my plans to move, but I also didn't know if it'd even matter to him. We were so flakey with one another already. Every time I drove home from his house, I'd listen to the same song over 'n over, *Good Man* by Third Eye Blind. I didn't see the relevance of it, I just couldn't stop listening to it. I sang it constantly. Months later, the lyrics would haunt me.

As soon as the season ended, I flew to Ireland with Ben, one of my best friends since preschool. We met up with another friend who'd already been living there for months, and then flew to Amsterdam, meeting up with another friend. We spent the last leg of our trip getting lost, riding river boats, and dodging bicycles. I remember when we first made it to our hostel in The Netherlands, I crashed for almost fourteen hours. My whole body ached and my eyes burned so badly I could barely hold them open. Ben could tell somethin' wasn't right, we'd been abroad long enough he knew it wasn't jet lag, but he never said anything. He only ragged on me for makin' us miss the free pancake breakfast downstairs the next mornin'. I'd had to crash early one night while we were in Dublin too, feeling like I had the flu, I could barely lift my head from the pillow, but it was gone the next morning, same as this time. I figured

I was just tired from not enough sleep and too many Guinness.

Jason had invited me over for dinner only a few days before we left for Ireland. I wanted to have a conversation about us *really* giving it a try this time, an *actual* relationship, and I felt like he had the same intention. I was shoveling pasta into my mouth as he sat across the table from me on his screened porch. He'd just started talking when I interrupted, spitting marinara with an anxious jolt, "Hey guess what! I'm gonna move to Tahoe at the enda the summer! I mean, not exactly Tahoe, I'll be livin' in Truckee, but basically!"

His face looked like I'd simultaneously punched him in the gut and handed him a bouquet. "That's *awesome*!" he said. He's always been nothing but sweet, overly sweet. He woulda been well justified in saying, "Ok but like what the fuck. You make no sense."

I'd get so upset when he locked himself away in the studio for hours, not joining us at the pub when I was in town, but then when he'd reached for my hand at one of his art shows, I'd pulled my arm away and spent most my time outside smoking. I didn't wanna embarrass him in case he wanted to appear single with all these people around him. *Especially* his family.

147

(Oh yeah 'n I'd accidentally *kinda* dated his brother for a very short time while I was still at the coffee shop… but THAT'S a whole other thing. Let's just agree, *I'm* as much at fault of sending mixed signals as anyone I've ever tried to date.)

After returning home from Amsterdam, I was back on that front porch swing. Dreaming away looking at the night sky. I was listening to Akon- *So Paid* and feelin' like quite the little hustler myself for all the money I'd put away that summer, the trip I'd just gotten back from, and the next one I was about to start. I had one week left to get all my warm clothes packed up for the Sierra Nevada's. I pumped my legs back and forth, swinging higher and higher, starting the song over one more time.

"Now come on girl, you need to go inside and pack! The dreaming's done, now go *do* it!" I heard my angels say.

"I wiiiiill I will, I'm just gonna swing a lil longer. One more cigarette." I sassed.

And with that, the chain broke from its bolts, and I came crashing down onto the porch! Stunned and a lil butt hurt. Literally.

"Geez! I get the message, I'll go pack!"

My dad had the chains fixed within forty eight hours, and I was back out there having my nightly conference call with spirit. Again, I heard, "Rebecca, come on now girl, you've *got* to pack! There is a time for dreaming and a time for doing."

But again, I put their call on hold, telling my angels, "I know I know I know, I'm just enjoying my swing and I wanna listen to a few more songs!"

My ass cheeks hit that porch so fast…

Dad came running out from the living room, "Don't tell me it just broke *again*! Those are brand new bolts!"

My mom had received that hammock as a gift when she was pregnant with me. She always said I would not stop crying unless she took me outside on that swing to rock me. It has withstood piles of cousins and dogs, swinging as high as we could for over twenty years, and it had never *once* broken. And now, in one week, I'd been dropped on my ass *twice* after clearly being told to get up off it.

No matter how skeptical I am, that was *quite* a coincidence. And it's never broken since. I *also* made sure I was on stable ground from then on when I decided to sass back at some divine guidance. Take note, your coccyx will thank you.

149

CHAPTER TEN

"I hate myself, doesn't everybody hate
themselves. I scare myself, but then I tell
myself that it's all in my mind."

Cursed Diamond

The Black Crowes

I had my pocket atlas and a long winded letter
I'd written to Jason tucked in my driver's door. Maybe
I'd use em later, maybe I wouldn't, but just in case. I
was fully stocked with water, boxes of Frosted Minnie
Wheats, and a bag of apples. I hadn't ever been big on
fast food except for my happy meals and taco bell when
I was younger. Those gahdamn cinnamon twists. Our
childhood bath salts.

I averaged around fourteen hours of driving a day, going through stacks of CDs and recounting everything I was driving away from. A statue I'd bought from Jason rode co-pilot. An iron poured figure of a woman, her eyes closed and her face turned upward, her arms spread open. Tears stream from her eyes, down her torso and into the earth. I had to have it. The first time I looked at this statue, my heart clenched tightly as if I could start sobbing.

It felt like, me.

I was holding my foot down on the accelerator driving as far across the continent and away from my failed attempts as I could. Even as elated as I felt, with the windows down, blasting Erykah Badu and making my way through Texas, I knew I was flakin' out on a lot of people, and a lot of situations. There was unfinished business I knew eventually I'd have to come back to. I could feel the cords stretching behind me the further I drove, like chewing gum stringing from the bottom of my shoes. It wasn't that I was gonna *stop* thinkin' about any of these lingering questions I'd never been able to answer, or the fear I couldn't fix, but at least I could do it from 3,000 miles away in an entirely new town.

Oh and I did. I put myself in a sort of isolated meditation retreat.

I didn't room with Shaunda and her boyfriend long after I got a job in Tahoe City. I kept waking up at night panicked. Bundled up on my yoga mat under piles of blankets, and a loud thumping would wake me, coming from the bedroom closet. My heart would race inside my chest and I'd sit up looking out at the snow, "It's nothing." I kept assuring myself. A few nights later, I woke myself up from screaming at the top of my lungs. I froze in silence,

"Was that, me?"

Then I heard Shaunda yell from their bedroom, "Becca...? Are you ok?" I was so embarrassed, I didn't answer her and we never discussed it. I knew it was time for my own place after that.

I rented my own little dollhouse of a cabin in Carnelian Bay. You could see the moon reflecting off the snow outside through the cracks in the walls, and the kitchen floor was so slanted you stood a good foot higher at the fridge than you did at the sink. I usually slept on the couch so I could be closer to the small heater in my living room, and did my nightly meditations in layered wool socks, a coat, and a warm knit cap.

It was perfect.

I became quick friends with Tracie, the receptionist at my new spa job. She rented out the cabin next door to mine, so we'd slide back and forth the well-trodden slope between our front doors. We had our morning coffee, evening wine, and long discussions on our families and love lives.

Every time I've moved, I've always been lucky to find these incredible friends. Women who are fiercely independent, genuine, and compassionate. I think we find each other when we need each other. Sometimes the greatest insight comes from people who don't know much of our back story. They can see where we are presently without the blurred context of our past.

I spent a lot of days hiking alone, walking in the snow, looking down at the sparkling lake and just crying happy tears. I was so overwhelmed with gratitude that *this* is where I was.

This is where I'd ended up after begging for my heart to be stopped, after spending every night sobbing and pleading with God to stop the pain. I'd tried so hard for years and years, to calm all the storms, to make sense out of all the lies and manipulations, my heart was so tired, but I held on. At seven thousand feet with significantly less oxygen than the tiny town I'd grown up in; I could finally breathe.

I could look down at my past the way I used to look down at our home from the back yard, perched high up in the boat tower. I felt a peaceful excitement bubbling under the surface, I was listening to my heart, following my *own* intuition, and it was working!

I sat having long discussions with my boss and owner of the spa, Sheryl, who lent me her collection of Dr. Wayne Dyer and Deepak Chopra cassettes. She sent me home with a boom box, excited to hear what I thought of the meditations, and I ate that shit UP. I played the seminar recordings nonstop, and never skipped my morning and evening meditations.

A couple weeks later, while bundled up like a snow angel slug in front of my space heater, I started hearing things I hadn't heard before on the recordings. I laid there with my eyes closed, quoting the words I'd now listened to for weeks straight, when I heard singing bowls. It was gorgeous, and with my eyes still closed, I noticed a choir of light beings walking through the doorway of my kitchen, and into my living room. The light poured into the corners of my closed eyelids, and I started to cry.

When I checked the CD the following day, of course, no singing bowls. Then, every time I'd go to turn on another recording in the afternoons, the play button would come popping back up. I stood there smashing it down over and over, giggling with frustration and amusement. I could practically hear the spirit next to me roaring with laughter every time I paused in suspense before quickly hitting it one more time. Playin' paranormal hot hands.

I then heard, "You need quiet, so you can *hear* us."

I brought the boom box into work the next day, so embarrassed I'd broken it after she'd been so kind to lend it to me.

"Sheryl, I am *so* sorry. I'll buy you a new one. I don't know what I did to it but-"

She plugged it in and pushed the play button as Dr. Wayne Dyer boomed from the speakers not missing a beat.

"Doesn't look broken to me," she laughed as my eyes rolled back in my head.

Oh what the eff y'all. Come on. That's just childish.

Now lemme tell you somethin' my spirit family, my soul companions, my unseen guardians, *whatever* you like to call em, are fucking hilarious, and they know it too. There's always spirits that kinda come and go for a season, just like any other relationship or friendship, but the lifers, the ones that've stayed from day one, they keep me entertained.

I've seriously worried numerous times, "Am I just fuckin' nuts?" But then others have experienced it *with* me. I know damn well these aren't actual people physically present in the room. Nor do I audibly hear their voice or feel harassed or unable to differentiate reality from non-reality (not that everyone would agree with me on that.) It's more of a presence in my heart, a thought or an impression placed in my higher mind that I can only feel if I'm tuned in, which has been *quite* a lot throughout my isolated porch swingin' life.

I asked as I journaled one day, "So, I've been stealin' y'alls material for a long time haven't I?" And as I felt them laughing and smiling they replied, "Yes, yes you have, but you're meant to! We're here to do just that! To assist you with those words, with those messages, that your heart already speaks so clearly. Steal away!"

Every time I've been in desperate search for teachers, for guidance, for someone to tell me what to do, they've repeated patiently, "That's why *we're* here.

To help you. To guide you and give you a clear channel of insight without it passing through ulterior motives and programming. Be still with your heart, breath into your joy, and you'll hear every word as clear as a bell."

I've always seen them as a choir of light beings. Always standing in a crescent shape when I greet them in the higher plains. I run to them in excitement, burying my face in their chests and wrapping my arms around them. I'm always extremely old, but with the appearance of a child. I can't help but cry even now as I write this. I've never felt such immense love, from a place I can't even completely make sense of myself, but when I see them, I know I'm home. I know they've never left, and are always surrounding me, celebrating every triumph, and holding me when I've felt alone and tired.

There are way too many synchronicities to even begin to fit in this book, but they *know* how to get my attention, I think *all* of our guardians do. They know exactly what it is that'll get us to look up from our distractions and acknowledge something bigger in ourselves, something we may have forgotten.

Now of course even after these long talks and realizations, that didn't mean that I stopped looking for outside guidance and validation like my enlightened life depended on it. Who, me? Drop me on my ass *twice* before I pay attention?

I'd taken a continuing education course a couple months after I'd graduated massage school, and been hooked on this particular healing modality ever since. The instructor and I, who we all referred to as Kumu, were in constant contact. I emailed her messages I received while sitting in my little cabin and she'd answer from her latest retreat in the Hawaiian Islands, "Once again, that was exactly what we were discussing! I shared your message with the class!"

Kumu said to me over the phone a few evenings later, "You're so brave to just drive cross country alone at your age-" and I cut her off saying, "Traveling and moving isn't scary to me, that's not the really big stuff, none of it's every really permanent. But the inside stuff, girls *that's* the permanent stuff, that's the stuff that scares the shit outta me."

At that time, I was *really* just trying to sound enlightened and insightful, to hear her say again how wise I was and get another gold star from my spiritual guru, but the next few months would prove my statement wasn't so far off after all. I was gonna be doin' a lot more traveling than I thought, and most of it, the scary stuff, the inside stuff, the permanent stuff.

Months later I had my tattered purple mat spread out on the living room floor as I did my nightly stretches and massaged my feet with castor oil. My phone rang and it was my sister,

"Hey Sissy!"

"Hey, um, have you talked to Dad?"

"Mmmm I mean, not recently, why?"

"Ummm alright well, there's somethin' I gotta tell you-"

My stomach hit the floor. I was used to hearing that phrase too many times.

"They just diagnosed Janice with breast cancer, and it's not lookin' so good."

Oh man. I rocked back on my heels and onto my butt, dropping my head in my hands, "Is Dad doin' ok?"

"I don't know, that's why I was wondering if he'd talked to you at all."

"No, but I'm gonna call him right now."

He answered the house phone with his usually tone, not sounding any different, but I knew he might be putting on an act. He filled me in on what was going on and I heard his voice slowly shaking.

"Dad, do you need me to come home?"

He took a deep breath and sighed, "I mean, if they'll let ya outta work."

I didn't need to hear another word. He's not one to ask for help like that so I knew I needed to put in my two weeks the next day and get the car packed.

I'd just sent him a hand written letter a few weeks before with The Avett Brothers CD. I wanted him to know I saw how much pain he went through as a kid, where he was neglected and overlooked, where he was told to toughen up and keep it together. I wanted him to know how sorry I was for hurting him throughout my growing years, and that I knew life had been hard on him, "Please don't let your anger stop your heart from feeling the joy of life Dad, there's so much to have hope for in this life and I don't wanna see you miss it. Those dreams you have, those sketches and blue prints, they aren't silly, DO IT! You deserve happiness!"

My landlord and boss, thank the Lord, could not have been more understanding. It wasn't even a full week and my car was packed to the gills, my house plants left to stay with their Auntie Tracie, and I was scheduled to be back at my old job in time for the start of the summer season.

This time when I made the drive, I was on a mission. I wanted to make the drive in four days so I could have time to unpack and get my massage room set back up for Memorial Day weekend. I was making good time so far and had already made it into Death Valley when a sharp burning pain hit the center of my gut.

I grabbed my abdomen, trying to keep my eyes open as I turned my hazards on and pulled to the shoulder. I was pouring sweat and tears welled up as I tried to slow my breathing. It felt like a hot poker was being pushed through the center of my stomach.

"Oh my God! I'm gonna die in the middle of Death Valley with Sting singing *Desert Rose*!!"

I punched 911 into my cell phone, but didn't hit the call button just yet. I didn't wanna overreact, and besides, I hadn't even passed a gas station in over an hour, how long would it take someone to get to me? How would I even tell anyone where I was!?

It's like calling your mom from the nurse's office only for no one to answer, and then you REALLY start crying. I didn't wanna solidify the fact that I might be found clinging to my boxes of Minnie Wheats alone in the desert weeks later. I sat up straight, shut my eyes, and pushed my exhales out forcefully, praying as hard as I could.

"Please take away this pain or at least let me make it to the next town!!"

And then after a few more strong exhales, the burning twist in my guts let go, and I was completely fine. I waited quietly to see if it reappeared or if I felt any resonant twinges, but it was gone. I turned off the hazards, and slowly climbed back onto the highway as the tires kicked up dust behind me.

I stopped to get gas outside Vegas, and the attendant asked where I was headed. Assuming he wouldn't know where my hometown was I simply said, "North Carolina."

"Hey! I'm from Mooresville!" He exclaimed, "Racin' country! What a small world!"

The friendly coincidence calmed my nerves a little bit. I didn't feel quite so far from home now, fearing I'd just cheated death by spontaneous combustion or, whatever the hell that was.

I continued making good time, only stopping for gas and snacks, but the ominous tone was still clinging to my nerves. I was coming through Arizona, passing another set of headlights only every hour or so, and staring up at the stars through my sunroof. I had the radio turned up playing *Closer* by Kings of Leon over and over, it seemed like a good haunting tune to compliment the other worldly feeling of driving those kinda roads at night. I wanted to make it as far as I could, knowing New Mexico and Texas alone would be about three boxes worth of Minnie Wheats.

Sam started texting my phone early the next morning, "Where are you? I'm lookin' at the weather channel 'n it looks like bad storms are gonna be comin' through Oklahoma and Arkansas."

"I'll be fine," I said, "I'm makin' good time, I should make it through Oklahoma City right ahead of it."

But she kept calling. "I dunno Sissy, it's not looking good, are you sure you shouldn't stop?"

"I'm on the home stretch, I gotta make it into town for the holiday weekend so I can go ahead 'n make tips to pay Dad back for helpin' me with gas money."

"I know but-"

"It'll be fine Sissy. I'm outta the real desolate areas now so if it gets nasty I'll just park at a gas station."

I made it about an hour outside of Oklahoma City when five white Dodge Rams flew past me with matching chrome roof racks and what looked like CB radio antennas.

"Those uhhh… are those storm chasers?" I thought to myself, startin' to sweat a lil now. I turned on the FM radio and heard, "If you're traveling east on I-40, please leave your vehicle and seek shelter immediately."

Uhh… uh oh y'all.

I looked at the horizon of stretching green fields ahead of me, clouds were bubbling up on either side of the interstate.

"I can make it, I'll just drive right through it before it hits town."

Then the next message over the radio was a live weather report. They were already experiencing baseball size hail in Oklahoma City. Shit. I might be able to dodge tornadoes but baseball size hail, not so much. Guess I better look for somewhere to pull over.

I spent the night at a truck stop, listening to the sirens go off and the local DJs begging people to stay off the roads that were underwater due to flash flooding. There ended up being 12 tornadoes that touched down, but to my surprise, no one really seemed to notice.

At every gas station I stopped, asking where a safe spot might be to park for the night, they simply replied, "Oh cause of the storm ya mean?" barely acknowledging the wall of black outside the glass doors behind me, "No honey, I don't know where to tell ya. Can I get ya anything else?"

Yeah some adult diapers and a Colt 45 would be great thanks.

Y'all don't mess in Oklahoma. Actin' like a handful of tornadoes is just a little afternoon shower. Nerves of steel.

As soon as the sun came up, I gladly hit the road and started the last leg of my trip. Get me the fuck outta *here*.

I made it two hours from home, and stopped to see Jason, we seemed to have our wires crossed. I got my feelings hurt once again, assuming he should know exactly what I felt. Now crumpled and sun bleached, I tucked the letter for him I'd been keeping in my car into the front sleeve of my Kahlil Gibran collection, and left it on his porch along with my copy of World War Z.

I picked up a pack of cigarettes, called my buddy Christa to meet me at Starbucks, and went to pick up the new Deftones album I'd heard coming through New Mexico.

Nothing had changed. I was still heart broken and bad at communication. Christa was, and still continues to be, my record holding coffee talk friend. As long as I can talk to Christa about it, I can get to the bottom of it, and the louder she laughs with me, the less of a big deal it becomes.

I was back at work twenty four hours later, pouring myself a cup of coffee and looking over my schedule for the day. Our boss and owner there, worked harder and with more heart than anyone I've ever met. I was happy to come in and do nine and ten hours of massages back to back. She'd come up to the receptionist desk at the end of packed weeks with a bottle of champagne, catching the cork in her stylist apron and shouting, "Way to go team!!!"

I made enough money to pay my dad back, and help him with the groceries and mortgage that month. The summer went by quickly and I boarded a plane for Kauai to attend an eleven day healing retreat with Kumu that September.

CHAPTER ELEVEN

"Still shackled to the shadow that follows you."

Sin

Stone Temple Pilots

*W*ithin days of returning from the retreat in Hawaii, refreshed, and ready to continue on my path, I had Christa cut off all my hair. I then packed up my car again, and moved myself further south. I'd really had my heart set on Charleston, but after a few friends had begged me to try Wilmington first, and I'd seen the Spanish moss and cobblestone streets downtown I thought, "I mean, this is close enough for now, sure why not!"

Now *surely* after attending all these healing retreats and practicing energy work and emotional release on every Tom, Dick, and Harry, I was ready to practice healthy intimacy and vulnerability with someone. At least without trembling, spilling things, and moving states away to see if the guy I was dating was really just being *nice*.

Denial can run so deep though, we can't even see the bottom. We can fool ourselves into studying healing and unconditional love with such obsession, that we bypass actually *doing* it for *ourselves*. Like feeling fine after three weeks on antidepressants and thinking, "Oh shit, I don't need these! I'm good!"

It's tricky y'all.

We may even quickly begin teaching on the very subjects that we're avoiding in ourselves, because then, to everyone else, we *got it*. We're overflowing with information and quotes from the masters. How many of us have taught about self-forgiveness, true friendship, and passionate love without *actually* experiencing it?

You can raise your hand, you're safe here.

Me too boo, me too.

The thing is, it's easy to get so excited about the wise words and fresh ideas sometimes; we forget to make sure they *actually* work. Ya know, by testing them on ourselves. Really.

We subconsciously continue self-neglect, passing the plate to the next person, and leaving ourselves unfed. We get so caught up spewing information as fast as we can, we don't step back to see if we ourselves are *actually* healing or if we've just put our pain on hold until no one's watching us.

I got an apartment downtown on the second floor of an old Victorian home. The exterior was covered in flaking red paint, now accompanied by layers of crunchy bright orange and yellow leaves falling from the cooling weather and recent storms. I could easily walk downtown to journal, sip coffee for hours alone, and smoke my American Spirits. I was healthier now, no more Camel Lights and Black 'n Milds. Still holdin' onto my habits yes, but hey, I was startin' to cut *some* toxins outta my life little by little.

I'd stopped eating dairy while I was out west, becoming so frustrated with the waves of cystic acne that were only getting worse. I'd sat on the couch, bundled up under my down comforter Tracie gave me, eating Greek yogurt with raw honey and raspberries, and quietly heard, "Ya know, why dontcha give cuttin' out dairy a try, just to see." And within a week, my skin was clearing up! I may be stubborn, but my vanity didn't ask twice whether that new practice was gonna

171

stick or not! I was gonna save thousands on concealer and new cleansers alone. Bye bye dairy!

I found a wonderful new job right off Market Street, at a small but cozy healing center with a sensory deprivation tank and an owner who I immediately loved. It was a small team of us that worked there, so we became close quickly and leaned on one another for advice with work and our personal lives. All of us seemed to be in the middle of transitions.

I was chest deep into my spiritual practice, following my Kumu down every rabbit hole, staying on the phone with her for two and three hours some evenings after we'd finished meetings or meditation with the group. I'd agreed to assist her teaching at a retreat in the south of France the following spring. Naturally, I decided I should go ahead and hike the El Camino while I was already out there, so I'd begun mapping out my starting point, train tickets, and the minimal previsions and clothing I'd need to get for that time of year.

After helping her teach a class months before, we sat at a restaurant, clinking our glasses over our upcoming trip to France. The space was rented, the deposits were being made, we'd done it! I couldn't have felt more accomplished and excited. I'd made enough money that summer that I could write my landlord a check for six months and put the rest of my money away for Spain in the meantime.

I never moved with much more than trash bags of clothes and a couple lamps, so my longtime friend Jay, who lived in town, supplied me with a couple chairs, and helped me pick up a small couch at Goodwill. This was the first time I'd moved in a long time, in which the town was new, but I had old friends there waiting for me. It was a welcome change.

I had a day dream before I found my apartment, that I'd find my people downtown when I played a song on the juke box. I'd turn on Primus - *My Name Is Mud*, one of my old favorites, and whoever started bobbing their head along, those'd be my people. That's how I'd know I'd found my kindred spirits.

Anthony, one of my new coworkers, asked if I'd meet up for a beer and give him some girl advice the second week I was in town. There was a sports bar called Drifter's just a few blocks from my place I wanted to try, so I told him I'd meet him there that evening.

I was about two beers and three chicken tenders into our therapy session, when I heard a familiar bass line thumping from the speakers, *My Name Is Mud*.

173

What the eff....?

I couldn't make out his face from the hood pulled over his head, but there was a tall guy leaned against the jukebox, sipping his beer and punching numbers for his next song, bobbing his head with the bass line. I wasn't listening to anything Anthony was saying, I froze thinking, "Wait, ok, but I thought *I* was supposed to play the song…"

I blinked, snapping myself out of my momentary paralysis, acting as if I hadn't missed a beat,

"Yeah yeah totally. Tell her if she wants y'all to have a serious relationship like y'all gotta be willing to make time for each other." Such wisdom.

Meanwhile I was internally screaming. No way was I gonna walk up to this guy at the jukebox and initiate conversation, uh uh, I let them come to *me*. Under no circumstances had I ever, nor *would I ever* lay *my* neck on the chopping block to be turned down. No no no. I much preferred having guys come onto me, followed by weeks of heavy flirting, and then I'd surround myself with male friends and stop answering my phone. It's a simple protocol, it had worked for years. Although I could not understand why guys didn't *see* I was in love with them and wanted to have a committed relationship. How much clearer could I make it? Friggin' idiots.

Needless to say I never spoke to the hooded mystery man that night, but I did finish my chicken basket and resolve Anthony's love life dilemmas, so, it wasn't a complete fail.

A week later when Christa and Jay came over for a girl's night, I saw it as an opportunity for further investigation of this hooded jukebox hero. Maybe I could get a better look at him, *not* that I told my girls my true intention behind picking that bar.

It was a chilly night, we walked in bundled up. We yelled around the bar, asking if we could turn the heaters on in the outside bar so we could smoke. He came around the corner in a black leather Air Force jacket, the collar pulled around his neck as he reached for his own pack of cigarettes from the pocket, "Heaters are outta fuel, I'm sorry, but I can zip down the canvas so it keeps the wind out."

So smooth, so nonchalant. I was already nervous and gassy. Great.

The girls laughed and made conversation, asking questions about the patches on his jacket and if his septum piercing hurt. He spoke softly with a low

175

baritone gravel, looking up to laugh and smile and I quickly looked down at my pint, taking enormous gulps and inhaling my cigarette like an oxygen mask.

He held his cigarette in the corner of his mouth as he pulled my next Guinness with such grit, such Sam Elliot masculinity. I was terrified. He'd leave us to our girl time and go back to cleaning the kitchen and I'd breathe a sigh of relief. My heart still races thinking about him that night, covered in tattoos and careless confidence.

We sat there with our boots up on the bar, cackling and slapping each other's knees, having our own private party until 2am. I fucking love those girls…. When it came time to settle up, he printed our receipts and Christa whispered to me, in anything but a quiet tone, "I'm leavin' him your number. He has been starin' at you ALL NIGHT."

"NO YOU ARE NOT" I screeched, digging my nails into her leg, "He's our bartender, and we're the *only ones here*! Where the hell *else* is he gonna look!? Dude do not embarrass me…"

She laughed, hysterical at the terror in my eyes, and promised me she'd leave it alone. When we made it out to the sidewalk, zigzagging with our arms wrapped around each other to stay standing, Jay said, "You

176

shoulda just asked him to come watch a movie with us. Ya know what, I'm gonna go ask him."

"DON'T YOU DARE!"

We raced down the sidewalk and back to the front door. I pushed her outta the way, swung it open and victoriously yelled, "HEY COME WATCH A MOVIE WITH US AFTER YOU CLOSE UP! I LIVE AT 555 GRACE STREET APARTMENT B. THE HOUSE IS RED. IT'S LIKE IT'S LIKE IT'S LIKE A VICTORIAN STYLE PLACE. WE'LL BE UPSTAIRS. JUST KNOCK ON THE DOOR. OK BYE!"

The girls were back outside trying not to pee on themselves laughing.

Thank God they didn't leave him my number. That woulda been embarrassing...

As soon as we got back to my house, I started snacking heavily on the leftovers of Beef Wellington I'd made us for dinner. The girls headed back down the stairs to grab the TV and DVD player from Christa's car she'd brought, knowing damn well I didn't own such worldly things.

I was three handfuls in when I heard them scream and come bounding back up the stairs, "HE'S HERE! HE CAME!"

"HUH!?" Crumbles of crust felt from my cheeks as I frantically looked for a cupboard to hide in. "Wait, is he still down there?"

"Yeah… Oh shit! We'll go let him in!" And they ran back down.

Suddenly all the alcohol hit and left my body at once, and I was struggling just to hold both eyes open at the same time. Great, now he's gonna think I had a stroke running back to the bar.

He came up the stairs carrying the electronics, and got everything set up for our movie as we ran around him frantic and squealing like intoxicated house mice. The girls sat on the floor, leaving the small loveseat for he and I to share during the movie. We joked and laughed until the sun came up and I decided it was time for him to go home.

I walked him down the stairs and out onto the porch, thanking him for coming over and setting everything up for us. He sweetly said, "I hope you have a wonderful day and thank you for having me," stood the collar up on his jacket, lit a cigarette, and turned to walk home.

I plopped back down on the bed as the girls said, "Well!?" I shook my head no, "He didn't even ask for my number, so, I don't think I'll be seein' him

178

again…but he *was* really sweet." I shrugged my shoulders feeling disappointed, "It was worth a shot."

As I write this, almost ten years later, he's in our bed pouring through the pages of his new Norse Mythology book. With his pillow tucked against the window sill and his feet hanging off the end of the mattress. I made sure to turn the fan on for him before I came back out to the living room to write. I know how he tosses and turns when it gets too hot. I left the door cracked so I don't startle him when I come back in. He only sleeps heavy if I'm already in bed next to him.

Ya learn those little things about someone day by day, the tiny pieces that make up the person you love beyond imagination. Two spoons of sugar and one good plunk of whole milk in his coffee. He likes to sing to me and slow dance when I'm in the kitchen, so I've learned to set timers so I don't burn dinner while my head's tucked into his chest. He only likes salt on his broccoli, while everything else gets pepper, *so much pepper*. He tells jokes in his sleep and rolls over just to kiss me and pull me across the bed. He'll never get sick of that one *Audioslave* album, and he knows every word to every song in *Sweeney Todd*. He never stops kissing my cheek, running his fingers through my hair, and smiling at me from across the room. "I'm so lucky," he

179

says, but it's really me. He says he's not all that smart, but he masters everything he does. He's effortlessly kind and he sings when he thinks no one's watching. He hears *Somewhere Over the Rainbow* whenever his dad's around, it never fails. He's scared the shit outta more than a few people. Removed someone's front teeth with a Louisville Slugger and punched out car windows, but when he laughs, he's a six year old boy, and I can't get enough of it. My dad said, "I imagine the boy's never seen the inside of a church," but he's shown me where God lives. He's held my hand while we've walked each other out of hell. Looking demons in the face side by side, terrified but desperate to save one another if it's the last thing we do.

I had no idea when I walked him onto my porch that morning that he'd rock me to sleep months later when my heart was breaking. That he'd teach me to sing again and take me to concerts just so I could dance. That he was the home I'd been running from and searching for for the last twenty years.

We don't often know who's gonna save our lives, and maybe we're not supposed to. Maybe the part of us that wants to give up, is better off oblivious. I think sometimes life knows it's been so hard on us, that if we don't get thrown a complete curveball, we won't take the bait. We'll sniff it out and run in fear.

Move to Pennsylvania. Move to California. Hike the El Camino. Protest no one could ever keep up with us. We're on a spiritual path and cannot be troubled by lesser mortals. We've learned everything there is to know about love, vulnerability, and soul connection- we don't need the practice.

What I didn't know, was that two weeks before I met Joe, before he played Primus on that jukebox and scared the daylights out of me, he'd washed up on Carolina Beach in the middle of a lightning storm, overdosing for the third time. He's one of the most passionate people I've ever met in my life, and his passion at that point, was heroin.

Shit's a slippery slope.

When there's a longing inside us, whether it be for love, validation, or simply relief from the mundane, if we're not careful, we can go searching for it and get tricked into believing we've found answers in some of the worst places. Even places that could very likely kill us. I did it through moving constantly and searching for enlightenment. He did it through opioids, which, for obvious reasons, is a tad riskier than being nomadic or into Deepak Chopra.

181

He crawled into my bed many mornings around five, after shutting the bars down and going to visit Liam across the street at the pub he owned and ran. They'd finally have their drinks and therapy sessions they'd offered the rest of downtown all night. The trees were just becoming visible from the suns light when I'd hear tires squealing, a radio blaring, and car door slam as his buddy Chachi drove up onto the sidewalk in a blaze, "Ahhhhh JOE!! Fuckin' love you man!"

He was managing two bars and working construction building a new parking garage for the school. He rarely slept, he just laid in bed, holding me, watching me sleep until his next shift started. Nothing in our lives or schedules made room for us to fall in love like we did, but we were head over heels for each other.

Something inside us broke open the moment we came together, acknowledging we'd made it, we could finally put our bags down and rest. It was barely two weeks into us dating and we were pouring pains out that we hadn't revisited our entire lives. I'd gotten news of a friend's mother passing one evening, a woman I adored and used to sing karaoke with every weekend back at home. I started crying and couldn't seem to stop. He drove me home, scooped me up from the passenger's seat, carried me upstairs, and tucked me in his arms tightly, "You just cry," he said, "I'm not goin' anywhere, so you just let it out."

I remember him climbing in bed a few nights later after a long night and a few whiskeys, and it was my turn to hold him while he cried. He sobbed and sobbed, while I ran my hands over his head, rocking him as he vocalized everything pouring out of him.

His friend Travis surprised him with a cellphone so we could text back and forth. We always messaged each other moments after separating for the day, "We're so lucky to have this while we can. We're just gonna enjoy every moment of it while it lasts." We both knew I'd be leaving for France in a few months and weren't sure exactly when I'd return. He was still busy partying and working three to four jobs at a time, but we still saw each other every moment we could. I lit up when I met him.

While I'd been packing up my little cabin to move back east, I journaled about my plans to move to Charleston, South Carolina at the end of the season. Meanwhile, Joe had put in for a transfer at his current job at Lowe's Home Improvement. He wanted to relocate to Mount Pleasant, just twenty minutes outside of Charleston.

183

Evidently we were gonna meet eachother one way or another. It seemed like we'd been connected for longer than we thought.

There was a single sunflower that bloomed far off from the highway going downtown. I'd looked at it every day I passed it, admiring it blooming all on its own, and then one afternoon it was gone.

I got to the bar to visit Joe and he ran to his car to grab me a surprise, and it was the sunflower.

"I saw it and just knew I had to pull over and get it for you." He said.

We were extremely open about everything from the get go, including our previous sex lives, or lack thereof in my case.

I had *never*, felt *that* when I'd slept with someone. I mean I'd barely felt much at all to be honest, but the first night we slept together, I saw my entire body light up like buttons on an elevator, and I thought, "*Oh* we're onto somethin' here."

We sat outside Drifter's having beers the next day, he let me know how many people he'd slept with, when he'd lost his virginity, weird things people had wanted him to try… he's a pretty open book this one.

"So what about you," he said, "probably got three waitin' on the side?" He laughed. "What's *youuuuur* number?"

"Including you?"

"Mmmhm."

"Uhhh…" pretending to count it out on my fingers, "Three."

He blew his cigarette smoke, making a face and shaking his head, "Hey that's not fair! I told you *my* number. I was honest!"

"Yeah so, unfortunately, I *am* bein' honest…" I laughed, "In fact, I could probably count the total number of times I've had sex *period* on both hands so…"

Having an exit strategy already scheduled and quickly approaching, I didn't bother to keep my usual walls up. I was just enjoying what it felt like to be completely, *embarrassingly* open with someone. At that point I thought it was still just a kind of experiment. We were just havin' fun. He was a bartender, and I was spending days with my phone turned off to go into silent meditation when Kumu came to visit.

Obviously this was just gonna be a fling.

So when Christmas came, I assumed there'd be no gifts exchanged. Of course when I showed up at his house after we both returned home from the holidays, he had a bag waiting for me, filled with everything I'd ever mentioned I liked, including avocados and papayas. He even bought me an album he thought I'd like from what he'd heard of my taste in music, *Them Crooked Vultures*. I mean he nailed it.

And I'd gotten him nothing.

I laid next to him in his bed that night, staring at the ceiling as he snored soundly.

"Oh my gosh, what the fuck, really? I get him *nothing*? I'm so in love with this guy, and does he have *any* idea. Please let him know how in love with him I am…"

As soon as the silent plea left my mind, Joe's snoring stopped, and he spoke as if we were in the middle of a conversation, "Is my love not enough of a gift for you?" and then went right back to snoring.

I sat straight up, leaning over his face 'til my nose was touching his, and stared at his closed eyes waiting for him to flinch. What, the fuck, was *that* sir?

An hour later, still wide awake, I was stressing out about a relative's health. I wanted to talk to him about all of my family struggles, but I also didn't wanna bowl him over. Again, he stopped mid snore and said, "I wish I could be there with you."

The next morning as he sat on the edge of the bed with his eyes still shut, I sat across his knees and asked if he remembered saying anything to me, but he had no idea what I was talking about. In fact he seemed as confused as I was.

This man, who *I* was supposed to fix, who I was supposed to teach about spirituality and enlightenment, saw into my life in ways I was afraid to even see myself. He sat on the end of my bed the first time he'd stayed the night, his eyes fixated on the full length mirror hanging on my closet door. "You know you've got a dark shadow following you," he said, with a twinge of familiar discomfort in his voice.

Days later, thinking I'd climbed back in bed after feeling the mattress depress behind him, he turned to wrap around me, but hollered for me when he saw an old woman standing there taunting him with maniacal laughter.

I assured him it was alright, these things had been pestering me for some time but they'd never caused any real trouble. He wasn't at all comfortable though, again waking up weeks later as I slept to see the old woman sitting next to the bed, watching over me, sternly stating that he was in *no way* getting rid of her.

He'd had darkness following him for quite some time. Eventually being validated for his visions after a roommate went into his bedroom, catching a glimpse of it and running out as quickly as he'd come in. Then shortly before we'd started dating, he heard something hit the pavement behind him as he walked home from work late one night. Turning to find no one behind him, he saw a small figurine laying in the street. After he and I realized we'd had many of the same experiences, he brought it to show me when we met for coffee one night.

I didn't like the thing at all, it felt sadistic and manipulative, much like the woman he saw following me. We got into a deep discussion about exactly what we'd seen in the unseen world.

"I mean, I've died a few times," he said, "and I can tell you, there's nothing over there. It's dark, silent, and cold."

His statement upset me, that wasn't at all what I'd seen having out of body experiences, I'd felt set free, greeting my spirit family with open arms! But then again, I knew he was just telling me the truth of what he saw. Both of our truths were valid. I'd seen the dark just as much as he had, but my heart hurt that he hadn't also seen the good stuff.

188

The stuff that doesn't startle you in the middle of the night, but holds you when you're afraid. The stuff that reminds you you don't deserve to be followed by the ghosts of your past, repaying generations of debt for the rest of your days.

Not that I'd completely learned that lesson.

With him I was comfortable talking about my shadows, the demons always one foot behind me, no matter how happy I was, there was always that gum stuck to the bottom of my shoe. He didn't just talk about it with me, he saw it just as I did, he felt the room change, he saw the lights dim, he held onto my hand acknowledging a presence when no one else did. We could just look at each other and smile, catching a shadow pass over the buildings downtown as we stood outside smoking, watching a world everyone around us seemed oblivious to.

I realized I'd never actually felt safe, not even when I was being fiercely independent. I was just sufficiently padded for protection.

I'd never felt safe enough to truly lean into love without a full face helmet and mouth guard, but with him, he was leanin' right back toward me. It didn't take much to completely trust and let go. For the first time in my life, I started wishing I didn't have to leave.

Then, not long after Valentine's Day, with the retreat quickly approaching, our space in the south of France suddenly fell through. The owner realized he'd double booked and Kumu called me in hysterics. All the deposits had to be returned and we'd have to push the date back at least a full year unless we could suddenly find another connection out there in the next six months. Now I didn't have a paid gig and flight to get started on the El Camino. I'd have to stay and let this completely vulnerable and life changing relationship continue to unfold.

Shhhhhhhit.

I gotta end it.

I mean I *have* to. We can't keep avoiding our lives just hiding away with each other forever, I gotta get back on my path.

I sat sobbing and journaling in bed the next morning, not telling Joe yet that I wasn't leaving. I was trying to figure out how to map out this new route.

"Is Joe gonna take me off my path," I pleaded, "I don't know what to do."

I heard a loud crash in my living room and ran out to see the painting over my fireplace had fallen, knocking the vase of roses he'd gotten me to the floor. The yellow and peach petals were scattered across the

190

carpet and I thought, "Well *somebody* wants me to call it off!"

I didn't stop to question *who* that was.

I sobbed into his shirt the next afternoon. He kept his arms wrapped around me softly as I explained to him between sniffles that it had been absolutely wonderful, I loved him with all my heart, but I didn't wanna keep him from living his life. I didn't wanna hold him back from meeting the girl that he could have a real relationship with. We were both on our own path and didn't need to hold each other back.

I'll never forget the way he looked at me, with absolute love and understanding as I kicked him in the balls. He wiped the tears from my eyes, telling me it was ok, and that I could come over and he'd just hold me whenever I needed him.

I didn't even want him to let go of me then.

I assured him I was fine, he needed to get to work and I needed to stop crying on his front porch. I made it home, dried my eyes, and called Kumu, letting her know I'd done it. I'd ripped off the Band-Aid and I was back on my path. "Good!" She said, applauding my feminist drive and determination.

I felt victorious for about four hours, and then quickly began regretting every word I'd told him, going into a full on panic attack. I wrote him a letter, admitting I was scared shitless and had no idea what I was doing, but I wanted to try if he'd let me. I snuck it into his army bag the next day, pulling up to his house to find he was packed and leaving town for a week to clear his head. I didn't think he'd be that upset about me calling things off, but realized maybe I wasn't seeing there were two sides to this pain. Oh. Oh man I'd really fucked up this time.

Finally reaching the bottom of his bag after a week-long bender, he found my letter and called me from South Carolina. He keeps that letter in his wallet, it's tattered and the ink's bled through the pages, but I still mean every word. He pulled the rug out from under me when we met, and we've never given up on each other since, not once, and it's never been easy.

The days and years that followed continued to get harder and harder, but we just held onto one another tighter. Untangling the knots, facing these monsters we'd run from for too long, and rocking each other to sleep.

When we stop running and decide to finally sit still with our soul, with the pain we've been stacking sandbags against our entire lives, everything tends to catch up with us at once. We need someone to hold onto when the tsunami hits.

CHAPTER TWELVE

"That secret that ya know, that you don't
know how to tell."

Blood Bank

Bon Iver

*J*ay and I were coming over the downtown
bridge, the sun was sinking behind the marsh
downtown as the lights sparkled down the river. My
phone lit up and I reached over to turn down the radio,

"Hey babe! We're comin' over the bridge right
now-"

His voice was only coming through in broken
syllables, the sound crackled and my stomach dropped.
I knew something was with him and I sat straight up in
my seat, "WE'RE ON OUR WAY. HOLD ON!"

195

As Jay and I's friendship goes, she somehow ends up being present for some of my most *woowoo* moments, even though, out of all my friends, she is as *non-woowoo* as they come! Always having a practical answer behind every synchronicity. She's my Bonnaroo buddy, my girl that shamelessly dances the Charleston with me at Snoop Dogg concerts and drag nights, and taught me how to drive a stick through the Blue Ridge mountains at four in the mornin'. But when it comes to paranormal shit… *not* up her alley at all. And *this shit,* was about to bowl a strike on the freaky scale.

We slid up to Joe's house and I was out the door running to him. He was standing in the yard, smoking a cigarette, white as a ghost.

"Where is it?" I said.

"I dunno, it sounded like the kitchen walls were breathing and then I opened my phone to call you and the screen had turned backwards and upside down. I don't even know how I managed to call you."

I marched up the steps and thew the front door open, livid that something dare think it was gonna fuck with someone I love! It didn't even occur to me to be scared for one second, I felt my army of guardians standing tall behind me, just as determined to call this thing out as I was.

196

As I entered, I felt the presence run for the back of the house. I quickly started following it, and a shrill woman's scream pierced down the hallway from Joe's bedroom.

I kicked the door open scanning each dark corner. I walked over to the window, tearing down the blanket he had hanging over it and pulled the blinds up to let the setting sun come in. I spun around behind me angrily, begging the little asshole to show itself. I yelled out the doorway to Joe,

"I want these skeleton and corpse posters OFF THE WALLS! These blinds stay OPEN and absolutely no more violent video games for the next month!"

I was *not* havin' it! You want these fuckers gone? You better stop leavin' out milk 'n cookies for em!

He was standing inside the front doorway by this point, his arms folded in front of him emphatically shaking his head yes to my demands. I followed him back onto the porch, giving one more look over my shoulder and down the hallway, "Try me bitch."

I wrapped my arms around him and apologized for goin' straight *Full Metal Jacket* on him, but I was *not* fuckin' around. I kissed him and took a deep breath, "We need a Guinness."

197

Now *that,* Jay was ok with, she's always down for a pint at The Dubliner. We sat down at the bar as stripes and solids cracked across the pool table behind us. Joe flipped his phone open and showed us the screen, still distorted beyond recognition. Jay nervously smacked her Parliaments against the bar, grabbing one from the pack and pinching it between her teeth, "Uh uh... I mean what the actual fuck y'all. I just don't... I can't...No m'am." Thankfully about an hour later, his phone went back to normal, but not before we vowed to toss it in the trash if it came up with some redrum or 666 messages. Oh haaaaail no we ain't textin no demons tonight.

I was yelling at myself as much as I was him about cleanin' up his room and realizing what kinda invitations he was sending out.

Just like we can leave the door wide open inviting defeating situations, energy vampires, and manipulative people, the dark forces come flocking to us just the same. Those friends that are always gettin' us into trouble.

When that kinda toxic love feels familiar, even comforting, we can fall prey to drunk dialing our old demons. We don't wanna let em go, just like an old relationship, we're not sure if it's possible or what it would even feel like to have healthy uplifting companions. To have connections that no longer supply us with the intoxicating highs and crashes of abusive people and substances.

Isn't it wild how we can reach so hard for what we think is love, or what we deserve, and somehow burry ourselves again. We can try and try, chasing what we think we fit into, but we haven't yet realized our <u>true</u> shape. We keep trying to squeeze into these old spaces where we once fit so perfectly, often suffocatingly so. Once we begin changing, there's a time of great discomfort. Nowhere feels like home anymore. We haven't yet found our true form, realizing it's in ourselves, that we have all the love and security we could ever need. That we encompass the ability to give and receive the compassion and love we've begged for all this time.

It's all at once excruciatingly painful and lonely, then absolute exhilaration as love begins pouring in. Depths of healing we never thought possible. Heights of hope and understanding we never knew existed.

I was realizing over and over that the manipulative stuff, the sabotaging stuff, usually made *quite* a ruckus to get my attention, while the empowering stuff patiently waited for me to pick up the phone. That whole respecting boundaries and free will thing works in <u>all</u> planes of existence, including the unseen spirits weaved throughout our lives. We aren't here to be puppets for anyone or anything, no matter how highly esteemed their credentials.

The "right thing", the thing that had been screamed to me through falling vases, so-called missed opportunities, and opinionated gurus, continuously shook me awake when my pulse had eased into a calming release. The louder these spirits and my Kumu yelled for me to stick to my guns, to never let *some man* pull me from my path, the harder my heart wept to please let me keep him. I was at war with myself, constantly sobbing in gratitude for this incredible soul that had cradled me without a moment of hesitation, and then becoming angry with myself that I'd give up years of independence, allowing someone else to sway *my* life decisions. It went against everything I'd believed, but he's good at pushing my buttons, at turning me to face myself, at saying things straight to my face whether I wanna hear it or not, and I'm good at receiving the bad stuff, the shaming, the blaming, I accept it with open arms and blistered feet. But the good stuff? Eh…

He knows how to find my places of discomfort in myself, the light, the places I've never been comfortable acknowledging, and he does it without looking away when I push back, without worrying I may be uncomfortable being loved with the light on.

I was driving us home from a Christmas party that first year we dated, he'd held onto me, bolstering me for the ninety minutes I made it wearing heals, then followed me to the car so I could put my combat boots back on under my cocktail dress. I'd tried to dress sexy for him but, I don't last long in stilettos, especially on cobblestone. "You are so beautiful," he said, as I nervously drove us down mainstreet, "and not beautiful like your mom might tell you, I mean you're *really* beautiful."

I couldn't look at him, but he never turned away, he kept his eyes on me until he knew I'd heard him, bolstering me until I was comfortable enough to take my shoes off, to stop blistering myself for not being what I perceived as desirable.

We often share dreams, and have the same past life visions. With my head on his chest one morning before opening my eyes, I could hear a low sleepy growl coming from deep inside him, so strong that I could feel it rumbling in my own chest, and his entire body was covered in thick dark hair. He felt to be near nine feet tall, but I had no reason to fear him, I knew he protected me as fiercely as he appeared to others, and I hugged him closer to me, holding onto the visions before it slipped away in the daylight. When he woke up and I told him what I saw, his eyes lit up and he shared his experiences throughout the years.

He'd been visited multiple times as a child by what appeared to be large wolves of men that only he could see, and then he had times where he himself became the wolf. A girl had broken his heart when he was in elementary school and he began scratching at the earth, ferociously howling and running through the tall grass on all fours. It hadn't occurred to him until he relayed this story that maybe this *wasn't* the usual response for an eight year old boy feeling heartbreak.

I held onto his hands, soaking up every word he told me. The way his eyes sparkled in comfort and acknowledgement of these visions he had vaguely shared before then tucked away for fear of judgement; I begged him to tell me more.

Being in love puts us in this incredible bubble of creation, of giving and receiving effortlessly, where *anything* seems to be attainable, because we're getting a tiny glimpse of the reality where it actually *is*. We don't need much sleep because we're running on magic. We see life through the invincible eyes we had as children, and this kaleidoscope of possibilities begins shining from within us. We can be anything, do anything, go anywhere. For those that love us, this is a wonderful sight to see, but for those controlling us, feeding on our failure, they couldn't be more disappointed or disapproving of our new found freedom. The dark clouds rolling across our rainbows become unavoidably visible.

Sometimes getting lost in a world outside of reason, can do more for highlighting the realities of our lives than any weights or scales ever could.

CHAPTER THIRTEEN

"Just because I'm losin' doesn't mean
I'm lost."

Lost!

Coldplay

*I*t was in the thick of winter and almost dark around 5 o-clock, I was driving into work and left a voice mail for my angels.

"So listen, obviously I'm not movin' anywhere anytime soon 'cause I am madly in love with this man, but y'all know I cannot survive on a nine to five with no adventures in sight. So, how bout I'll go wherever y'all want me to go, if y'all could just send me somewhere."

Twenty minutes later, my first client who'd been coming to see me for the last year, offered me a full paid trip to Belize. He'd gotten a casita right on the water and had a friend coming to paint murals with his fiancé, and wondered if I wouldn't mind coming along to do some massages.

Our session came to a close and I ran down the hallway in excitement, ready to text Joe the great news, and there was a message waiting from Kumu inviting me to teach in Kauai the following October, fully paid.

"Two in under two hours!?!? Ok that's a record!" I thought, "I am on a *roll* now."

There's something about good news that shines a spotlight on the people who are nauseated by our happiness.

My sister Samantha and Kumu both separately warned me I was in serious danger, I didn't need to be going to some third world country with some man I barely knew. I appreciated them being worried, but I also knew, if it was *them* who'd been invited, they'd never have asked for my opinion.

There's a thin line between honest concern from a place of love, and the need to control someone else's life by planting seeds of doubt and fear in their own judgement. Ya know what though, your gut *always* knows the difference. It knows when someone just likes to habitually rain on your parade doesn't it? I bet there's at least one person you can think of right now, that if you called em with good news, they'd somehow turn the conversation into a lesson about your gullible positivity complex.

What's funny is, they both separately said the same things, "I'm just looking out for you. I don't think you understand like you *think* you do." Condescendingly protecting me from my easily manipulated and naive self. I'd heard those phrases my whole life, and they'd never seemed to do much but make me miss out on what I really wanted, always telling me to just get back in bed, give it up kid.

Now, as I write this, Joe and I've just returned from our second trip together to stay at that casita. That man, that they warned me couldn't be trusted, has opened his home in paradise to us without hesitation. Years after he'd first invited me, I spent months at doctor's offices, maxing out credit cards and dropping to ninety-five pounds, and he again welcomed us to go stay, relax, and recharge without a second thought. Despite the betrayal and deceit we were experiencing left and right, this man reminded us of the good nature and warmth that continues to exist around every corner. He reminded us the world is an abundant place, no matter how desolate it may feel at times.

I moved in with Joe as soon as I returned from that first trip to Belize. It was time to take a chance, and just as that trip later proved to be, what may appear as foolish and risky to the world, may actually be wise investments in our future, we just have to stop listening to everyone else's opinion on the matter.

My mom had moved back down south from Pennsylvania to North Carolina, almost exactly two hours from where Joe and I were now living together off of Market Street. We'd meet once or twice a month for lunch, I'd go there and we'd walk around downtown to grab coffee, or she'd drive down to me and I'd take her out for a bite on the Riverwalk. I really enjoyed it, even though admittedly some days it was exhausting, I just missed my mom, and I never stopped romanticizing that maybe this visit would go better, maybe things would change. Even if it was just a few good moments, a short highlight reel, I missed *that* mom, and I kept digging to find her.

The conversations were usually depressing stories about what really happened between her and my dad, her daddy leaving and never returning when she was a child, her relationship with her mother, and why her heart's been broken for so long, but I still miss those talks with her. I miss being close with her.

A connection is a connection, even if it's funneling the life out of you, and that's all I wanted, was to keep a connection. I always sat there nodding my head, hoping one day the roles would reverse and she'd say, "Well I've been talking about myself long enough, what about you?"

We sat outside her local coffee shop for going on four hours one afternoon as she went over the same stories I'd been hearing for thirteen years, but I listened. I always listened. That day, she decided to tell me what really happened before pressing charges against Charles so many years before,

"You know what your daddy *did* don't you?"

"I mean, I heard he got his revolver 'n was heading to Grandma Fran and Charles's house but Uncle Terry stopped him-"

"Oh Rebecca," she shook her head, "he drove out there to make a *deal* with Charles!"

"Huh?"

"Rebecca, your daddy, who says he loves you girls so much… told Charles he'd hold off on pressing the abuse charges, if he agreed to supply the lumber for the new house. See, Charles ran a lumber supply business, and *your daddy* saw an opportunity to save some money. Now tell me *that's* not a man who's cold to the core."

I was so used to these kind of psychological tornadoes from both my parents by that point, that I just calmly shook my head in disgust. Acting unimpressed, and filing it away in the usual folder to decide later if it was even true or not, which, let's be honest, really just meant that I planned on crying about it in private at my earliest convenience.

When Joe got home from work that night, I was lying in bed doing just that. He laid down and curled up behind me as I told him what my mom had said to me during our visit, sobbing into my pillow. I just couldn't mentally and emotionally handle anymore, and I'd already been saying that for ten years. Every time I reached my breaking point, I somehow managed to dig down even further, somehow it always managed to get worse. Every story and action in my family kept adding up to a reality I just couldn't face, and even now, would rather not most days.

I cried at the thought of my father, my protector, seeing a financial opportunity in his own children's molestation. I cried that my sister and parent's voices sparkle with excitement every time they share a story that they know is going to devastate me. I cried because my heart was exhausted from trying to make sense of it all for so long.

Joe didn't say anything. He just pulled me closer, kissing my cheek and rocking me back and forth singing, "Here comes the sun, doo doo doo, here comes the sun 'n I said, it's alright…"

Whatever blissful ignorance I had left, ran out that day. Something just broke.

He'd quit bartending and our routines shifted from him coming home at 3am, to us waking up at 4am for him to go do masonry work at the army base two hours away. I'd come home in the evenings dragging, brewing a pot of coffee so I could get dinner going for when he came in the door exhausted from being in the rain and wind all day building scaffolding.

My body ached so badly some evenings, I hugged him, showed him his dinner plate, took a hand full of probiotics and climbed back into bed. I felt weak and clammy most days, constantly fighting off what I thought was a cold or the flu. I had a week that I felt especially feverish and lethargic, so I just kept myself dosed up on Alka-Seltzer Cold & Flu until my body got over whatever it was I was fighting. I didn't realize it had been almost ten days pushing through until Joe said something when I came out into the living room,

211

"Babe! Your neck is swollen."

"It is? Can you look down it?"

He grabbed his flashlight and leaned forward as I stuck my tongue out ready for the diagnosis, "Ahh! Babe you've got like, a puss pocket on your right tonsil!"

"EW! A wha!?"

"You are <u>not</u> goin' into work. I'm takin' you to see a doctor."

After being told I must be suffering from amnesia because I *most definitely* had one of my tonsils removed, whether I remember it or not, and was for sure suffering from a bad case of strep throat… (Insert heavy eye roll) No matter how many times I told him my throat didn't hurt, the doctor kept saying, "Popsicles will help with the pain." I wanted to scream.

I returned to the waiting room pretty defeated.

"So what'd he say?" Joe sprung from his chair.

"Uhh… that unbeknownst to *me* and the rest of the medical community, I am missing a tonsil, aaaand after swabbing my throat with a long q-tip, and I quote, saying, "Ew." … he, threw the q-tip in the trash, and said I have strep."

"So, you just, lost a tonsil somehow…?"

"Evidently so… Let's just go get these antibiotics. I feel like a man that was just told he's missing a testicle… musta blacked out and left it at a house party or something…"

I took my antibiotics religiously, and every morning, I cried when Joe looked down my throat with the flashlight (clearly seeing two tonsils mind you.) and it wasn't getting any better. I'd had enough of that. By the fourth day, I decided the antibiotics weren't gonna do anything as long as there was still a puss pocket on my tonsil, so I grabbed some medical supplies from the kitchen and got to work.

After my quick surgery, I minced up 3 cloves of raw garlic and shot em back with a cup of water, and by that afternoon, I was already feeling back to my old self.

Joe called on his way home to ask how I was doing.

"SO much better babe, I got ridda the puss pocket and started takin' raw garlic."

"Wait, how'd ya get rid of it all of the sudden?"

"It wasn't bad, I just held my tongue down with a spoon so I could see it in the mirror, and scraped it off my tonsil with a butter knife."

213

He was gagging and yelling by the time I said scrape, "BABE! Ohhhhh my…"

"It's already better though! The antibiotics ain't gonna help if they're just fightin' the puss pocket!"

I could feel him shaking his head over the phone, "UGH! Baaaabe…"

A day later, I was back to work and doin my seven hours of massages, and a few months later, we moved again to a studio apartment closer to my job. As exhausted as I was, feeling like I had the flu two and three times a week, my Alka-Seltzer intake so regular my farts should've been fizzing, I genuinely loved my job. The people I worked with had me laughing and excited to come in every day, and the experiences and connections with each client were so wonderful.

Things in the background were making a steady downward spiral, but I kept my laces pulled tight, holding onto Joe, and the joy and hope I was experiencing at my job, and steadily in myself.

I continued to journal for hours a day, giving myself my two hours before I had to get ready for work to visit with my spirit family and collaborate on our insights. As my mom's mental state was rapidly declining, I began to question my own even harder, terrified I was witnessing what was to come for me. As

I always have, I got pretty stubborn and insistent with my unseen pit crew, demanding they make themselves known or I was gonna tell em to kick rocks.

"Look, if I'm *not* crazy, and y'all really *are* with me constantly, I need to see somethin' that I can't just make up in my own mind. I wanna see, (thinking of the most outlandish manifestation possible) some BUBBLES. Yeah, show me some gahdamn bubbles."

Then, 48 hrs after so sweetly demanding some "gahdamn bubbles," my mother came to town with a box of re-gifted VHS tapes and newspaper clippings for my birthday. As I tried to act excited over newspaper clippings of recipes for banana nut bread from 1997, she pulled a bubble wand from her purse and began blowing them directly into my face.

Well played.

As the bubbles popped and splattered on my eyelashes and cheeks, I could imagine them laughing hysterically, "Any more brain busters ya lil asshole?" What better way for my answer to come through, than from the last person I expected, but that's always how those answers seem to show up don't they. The last person or scenario we ourselves could ever imagine, and there it is, just in case we thought we were making it all up.

I think when life seems to be crumbling below our feet, those are the times our ancestors and guides know we need magic in the worst way.

Days later, I stood in our kitchen after having another defeating family phone call, I could feel multiple spirits just hangin' around, chillin' with me as I chopped vegetables for dinner. I set down the blade for a second, and again questioned, "Is someone really here? Am I really sensing, what I *think* I'm sensing all the time?" I waited in the silence, and then my phone, which was sitting across the counter, lit up, and began playing Coldplay- 42.

I'm not even gonna tell you what the lyrics are, I'll just let you go play it right now so your eyes bug out just like mine did.

Go ahead, I'll wait right here.

....

Right?

Did you pee a little? Cause *I* peed a little. I was like, "OK BUT HONESTLY…" I was lookin' out to the living room like, "Ok y'all…look, that was a *little* sassier and freakishly specific than mama was expecting."

And so it continued. The little flashes, the insights and gut feelings I'd had my entire life, started

216

to interlace its fingers with my everyday life until there wasn't much separation left.

I had clients trying to catch me playing tricks on them, quickly raising their head from the cradle, absolutely positive I was pouring warm oil onto their sore shoulder, and I'd laugh still standing at their hips or legs, same as the last time they checked.

I'd never been certified in Reiki, and I'd even missed the only days spent on teaching energy work in massage school because I'd left for my sister's wedding, so I never really felt comfortable saying I practiced energy work specifically. I'd usually refer clients to someone who had the legitimate certifications. I was just wingin' it.

A woman who was accidentally scheduled with me when our receptionist misheard her request, became progressively agitated during her session.

"I've never had someone pull energy from my feet like that," she barked sharply, "and *I'm* a Reiki Master…"

"Huh…" I said, feeling like I'd accidentally insulted her somehow, "well, ya know, those exhaust pipes can always use a lil clean out." I wasn't *tryin'* to pull anything outta anywhere I was just, where I thought I should be.

217

She continued making remarks throughout the entire session about the heat she felt coming from my hands, and not in a nice way. It was as if she was checking my pockets for shoplifting.

Afterward I greeted her in the hallway, and with an arched brow and a stern face, she instructed me on where I should go to receive training and proper certification as *she* had. That is, if I wanted to understand what it was I was doing...

Thanks! Is that also where ya got that holier than thou attitude? Yeah, Ima pass on that. I get enough salt in my diet from corn chips and peanut butter pretzels, but have a good one!

Not surprisingly, a week later I had a woman sent to me specifically for energy work. I let her know we'd be making it up as we went along, which she was completely comfortable with. I spent the majority of time on her abdomen and she, like my other clients, was raising her head to see where my hands were.

"Have your hands been on my chest?"

"Nope, still on your abdomen."

"That's so strange, I keep feeling hands right over my heart."

I laughed and shrugged my shoulders, "I only got a set of two so evidently some help's steppin' in."

218

I felt the energy move from around her diaphragm and up toward her sternum, and finally into her heart where it began to dissipate and breath again. I heard a man's voice in my mind say, "Tell her she can talk to me anytime she wants."

"God?" I asked. Hmm, didn't recognize him.

I was quietly walking around the table to grab her a tissue when I saw her begin crying and she said, "What *was* that?"

"Well, *somebody* wants you to know you can to him anytime you want."

Then she really started cryin', and then of course I started crying and pulled up a chair, grabbing the whole box of tissues. She took a couple deep breaths and held my hand,

"We're holding a celebration of life for our son tomorrow."

I was lucky to work on her one more time after that, to see her filled with peace. She held onto my hands again and said, "I pray to God every night that you can continue to share this gift."

I hope she knows that every time I doubt myself, every time I think, "Who the hell am I? I don't even know what I'm doing." I think, "but… she said that prayer just for me, and I wanna hold up my end."

I still have no idea what I'm doin really, but things always seem to manifest as they need to, our spirits are highly intelligent that way, they don't need much instruction, just hands to hold. I'm too stubborn for much instruction anyway. Spirit knows I like to learn from experience.

Weeks later a dear friend allowed me to borrow her healing room for a private session so I could work on a fellow employee. There's a Hawaiian chant very close to my heart that I like to sing but can't really do too often at the spa, so I was really excited! Before I started the chant, I told her to please invite anyone she wanted to be present for her session.

At the close, I was knelt down at the crown of her head while she laid face up, with my hands placed gently over her heart. I felt a cool breeze touch the bottoms of my feet, and a tall figure come and stand right behind me. He placed his hands directly over mine, and as I asked who he was, I felt a gentle baritone, "Michael."

Tears streamed down her cheeks as I slowly lifted my hands to end the session, and she asked, "Does *everyone* get to feel love like that?" I smiled at her, crying myself, and shook my head no, that was just for her.

We sat to have a cup of tea afterward and get our bearings as she told me how she was feeling.

"Ya know, I invited Archangel Michael." she said, and then it was my turn for the water works.

"Girl he came. That was him you felt."

These experiences, these peeks into the world that we're constantly swimming through but rarely notice, it kept me going. The worse the nightmares got, the tighter my jaw clenched and hands shook, the faster my mother's mental health became, the harder my spirit family cracked jokes and reminded me to dance and sing. One literally began dancing around me during a massage one day, begging me to never lose my faith in miracles, "Heck, buy a lottery ticket! Do it TODAY!" they exclaimed, "You've got to believe!" I kept hearing Frank Sinatra singing, "Fairy tales can come true it can happen to you…" for the rest of the day. Singing the entire lyrics to myself, I realized how much I'd needed to hear it. It's always been one of my favorites.

When I was pushing my shopping cart of groceries out of Lowe's Foods that evening, I crept up to the Mega Millions kiosk, but realized I had no idea how to even fill out a ticket, I'd never done it before. I buckled my seat belt after loading the car, admitting I'd chickened out, and asked, "Ok look, how bout, if like, y'all could just have someone *gift* me with a ticket? Technically I'd still be playin right?" Then I forgot about the whole ordeal and went home to start dinner.

Joe stood next to me at the kitchen counter, emptying his pockets from the day, loose change, receipts, candy bar wrappers, and a green scratch ticket. My eyes widened.

"Yeah so, kinda random… I stopped at the gas station to get a drink and Reese's cups, and the teller just handed me this and said to give it to my wife. So, here ya go…"

I immediately began slapping him in the arm with it and screaming like a lunatic.

"ARE YOU KIDDING ME!?"

Now I wish I could say I scratched that ticket and we're now livin' lavish but I think I got all of three dollars, but that didn't even matter. I was beside myself. He kept laughing at me bouncing all over the kitchen in hysterics as I got dinner ready. Then as he made is way up the stairs to take a shower, he began whistling, "Fairy tales can come truuuue it can happen to yoooou…"

Be. Side. My. Self.

Y'all. I hadn't told him about the song either.

222

I can't. Even now I'm like WHAT SORCERY
IS THIS!?

Hope is an incredible thing, tied to the the end
of a string, it floats high above the tree line. From
ground level we may be in the thick of it, we may be in
the middle of the battle field, but our hope shows us
there's a way out, a place to breathe freely high above
the smoke and the smog.

At our weakest moments, when all we can
manage is to not lose grip of that tiny string, it's very
often the thing that keeps us going; that turns our gaze
away from despair.

CHAPTER FOURTEEN

"How much of my mother has my mother left in me, how much of my love will be insane to some degree."

In the Blood

John Mayer

*A*midst all these tiny miracles, intertwined with all these hopeful moments, I was clenching my jaw just like I had as a child, waking every night from the same horrific dreams. Constantly running and hiding from violent attacks, watching people fall to their death, shot point blank, and hiding, never to be found. If I didn't wake from being killed myself, I woke with this crushing despair that once again no one came, no one tried to save me. I was alone, hopeless. I'd roll over to hold onto Joe's arm, tucking my head into his chest to calm my racing heart.

My mom was beyond help, we'd tried and tried for years, but she constantly found a way to sabotage anything done for her. She kept telling us before we'd leave her house,

"I'd kill myself but I don't have the guts."

Sam would be having twins soon and need to take care of her own family. I was beyond exhaustion.

We'd sat with her for hours on end, for months at a time, trying to help sort out her finances,

"Mom, what if we got you into a townhouse? Your cost of living would be so much lower, you wouldn't need to pay for someone to mow anymore. You could even put some money aside for the boy's college- "

She interrupted with a groan, shaking her head at the very mention of putting money away for the kids. At that very moment, she was wearing a sweatshirt she'd bought herself which read, Proud Granny.

I got shamed a lot for overlooking an obvious case of Dementia or early onset Alzheimer's, for being a cold and impatient daughter. "Oh Rebecca, your mother's *such* an angel, I know it's so painful to watch someone you love change," they'd say in emails, and I wanted to *scream*.

"She *hasn't* changed, not at all. *That's* the point. She's been like this since before I was even born!" But nobody wants to hear that. Nobody wants to believe they were fooled.

People don't wanna hear that what we call monsters, are really just the worst versions of ourselves come to life. Most people don't wanna believe in monsters in the first place. They don't wanna believe that *that* kind of darkness could slip past everyone's judgment and sit right next to them, not only undetected, but praised for its angelic nature.

I drove the two hours after work and straight to the grocery store, panicked one day after she'd told me she had no food and wasn't eating. I filled the cart to capacity, making sure she had at least a month's worth of groceries, only to open her freezer and see there wasn't even room enough for the frozen peas.

"Mom. I thought you said you weren't eating because you had no food."

"Rebecca, there's nothing I like in there."

Not long after that, a relative took her shopping for a new wardrobe after she'd evidently eluded she was wearing nothing but a bathrobe. When I saw her

227

afterward, I mentioned the shopping trip and what a treat it must've been. She rolled her eyes and moaned, "Yeah well, not really. It was all from Walmart."

I thought about her cornering me in the kitchen so many years before, letting me know I was high maintenance.

I'd started having a vision of her that was constantly flashing through my mind for months. I'd run into her home, racing around the corner into the kitchen to find her covered in blood that wasn't her own. I'd look at her and say, "Mom. What have you done?" then I'd see blue lights from cop cars pulling up outside her kitchen window.

I didn't share the vision with Joe, my mom gave him the creeps enough already. I'd already promised him we'd <u>never</u> stay over at her house. He was scared she'd try to kill us in our sleep, so was I. My own mother had made me cringe my entire life. Her kisses on my cheek always lasting a little too long, her hugs feeling like I could crawl out of my skin. The older I got, the more I just allowed myself to pull away sooner.

Shortly after moving into our new studio apartment, I made a new friend that lived three doors down from us, Dusti. God love her, she talked me through so many of the ordeals with my family that next year, giving Joe a break from the constant bombs dropping. We'd meet for our evening tea chats and it was like we'd been friends all our lives. I love those kinda people, who have nothing to hide and everything to share. Once again, I'd moved and found another friend. They're hiding out everywhere y'all, just waiting for us to sit down for tea.

She gave me a quick pep talk one afternoon before I left for a dinner with my mom, sister, and brother in law.

"You got this girl, but just in case, you know I'll have the kettle on when you get back. Or wine, if that's more the speed!" Dusti holds the tent up for a lot of people if ya know what I mean. She's the girl ya wish ya had every night you drank too much and needed someone to get you home safe.

I was hoping I'd be able to just swing by and pick up Mom on the way to the restaurant, but she called when I was an hour out to let me know Sam wanted to push back our reservation.

I walked in the front door and her sleigh bells jingled quietly, the ones she's always hung at every main entrance. The house was thick and stale with the smell of unwashed dog, pee stains, dirty dishes, and clouds of Jessica McClintock perfume.

229

I used to spray that perfume all over my ball gowns when we played dress up. Wearing full length gloves and imagining I was Josephine March, in love with the handsome warm hearted professor, standing up to the lions of injustice.

She hollered from her bedroom to make myself comfortable, she was just getting herself ready until we heard back from my sister about a time for dinner.

I sat on the couch and barely ten minutes passed before I was salivating from nausea. Sam called and let us know it'd be another hour and I wanted to cry. I wanted to turn around and go home already.

I did my best to hide my seasick face at the restaurant. I didn't even wanna mention the word vomit in front of Samantha, her first trimester had been pretty rough. I slowly chewed on three bites of food and tried to think about anything but my gag reflex. We paid our tabs, hugged goodbye for the night, and mom and I left to take her back home before I started the drive back to Wilmington. I was feeling so ill by that point my eyes were welling up with tears. I wasn't sure I'd even be able to make it home. I'd texted Joe during dinner, "It's getting worse, I'm gonna try and make it but I might have to stay here, I'll let you know."

As soon as we got back to the house, I went to pee and put some cold water on my neck while Mom changed into her pajamas.

"You like Mama's Jammies?" She said, posing in her bedroom doorway.

In that moment, I felt someone saying, "Are you paying attention Rebecca? Pay attention." But I wasn't sure what I was supposed to be looking for.

She told me to drive safe and kissed my cheek. I tucked my neck into my shoulders, trying not to let her notice, and told her I'd text her when I got home. Just the sight of her in pajamas had always made me sick to my stomach, I felt awful for being so repulsed by my own mother. How could I feel like that? About someone who raised me and loves me?

I cried behind the steering wheel, buckling my seat belt and praying the food poisoning or stomach bug or whatever it was could just hold off until I made it back. I could get there in an hour and a half if the traffic wasn't bad.

About twenty minutes down the road, the bright lights from a familiar gas station lit up the dark asphalt, and I realized my nausea had lifted completely. Again I heard, "Are you paying attention?" Then a scene flashed into my mind. We were at Fran and Charles'. It

231

was early in the morning. I was still young enough I was barely walking, and Mom was in her pajamas holding my hand. She was walking Samantha and me down the hallway into Charle's bedroom.

I felt my mother's sense of accomplishment, of pride in herself for making her parent's happy. Instead of shock or anger when I saw this quick vision, I felt nothing but peace and clarity. This sobering understanding of the truth behind our sexual abuse from a bird's eye view.

"Oh my God," I thought, "If this is real, it's been rotting inside my mother all this time. It's why everything always leads back to the abuse, why she's never been able to let it go and move forward. It's why she apologizes to us every day, but we can never forgive her enough for her to stop saying it. That's why the sight of her in pajamas makes me sick."

A week later I invited her to come down for a coffee date. I needed to see if there was any validity to what I saw. Maybe I was only picking up on her guilt from not catching the abuse in time? Either way, I knew I needed to get answers if I had the chance.

We sat at a private window side table. She hunched over her cup, the corners of her mouth hung heavy, carving deep creases as she picked at her cinnamon scone. I leaned forward and did my best to keep my tone warm and inviting, approaching her like a therapist asking a child why they feel the need to abuse the neighbor's cat.

I explained to her what I saw in the vision, and I also told her the sense of accomplishment and pride I felt associated with it.

"From the perspective I saw Mom, *even though* it was a horrible thing, for the first time in your life, you felt you'd finally made everyone happy. Your husband was in the kitchen with your mother, your step father was pleased with you... everyone was happy with Beverly."

She picked her head up slowly to meet my gaze, not blinking once. The creases softened. She looked through me with a steady flat line,

"Yes Rebecca. How could you *know* that?"

Her eyes widened as if I'd solved an impossible riddle or magic trick, not discovered the truth about our molestation. She sounded relieved to be understood, thankful that I finally saw she's only been trying to get what's rightfully hers.

The eternal victim.

233

A perfect illustration that narcissists, sociopaths, and psychopaths are nothing but children forever fumbling at a Rubik's cube, twisting and turning people's lives to get what was denied them. Treating others as mere numbers in their mathematical calculations. It's a protocol that lacks any sense of humanity or reasoning, they learn to fake it instead. Even the most malicious acts are seen as well deserved, as just part of the game. In a mind like that, everyone is in debt, because no one has suffered like *they* have suffered.

No one.

Not even their own children.

She blinked a few times, and went right back to her snack, like a toddler not able to grasp the magnitude of her parents announcing their divorce.

I sat back and watched her, far enough from who I'd thought she was, that I could simply observe now. Where *was* my mom, had she ever even been in there, or had I just imagined who I needed her to be all my life?

If the vision had been about something in the last decade, maybe I could have accepted it easier, but this was who she'd been since I was born. This was my whole life.

There was a late afternoon when I was living in Pennsylvania, I was driving us back up the mountain as the sun was just starting to set. I stared ahead, squinting at the road, letting my foot off the accelerator for each curve, then punching it uphill to highlight my rage,

"MOM I AM SO TIRED OF YOU GOING OVER EVERY DETAIL, EVERY DAY, ALL THE TIME FOR YEARS AND YEARS! OUR ENTIRE LIVES HAVE BEEN ONE THING AFTER ANOTHER! I CAN'T HOLD ONTO EVERY SECRET OR ASSUMPTION YOU'VE MADE ABOU-"

"REBECCA! YOU DON'T *KNOW* WHAT I'VE BEEN THROUGH WITH YOUR DADDY! AND *MY* DADDY LEFT ME! YOU DON'T EVE-"

"I GET IT! I FUCKING GET IT OK! I'M JUST… tired Mom. …I'm tired of getting pummeled every day. I can't fix-" I started to lose steam as she interrupted me.

"But Rebecca, what about *me*? What about your mommy? I never-"

Her voice stopped mid-sentence as the beginning keys for *Head Over Heels* by Tears for Fears came over the radio. We both went completely silent. She leaned across enemy lines to turn the volume up as

235

we respectfully postponed the argument until the song ended. We turned and looked out opposite windows, singing every word with our fists clenched, still scowling. Just two heartbroken kids screaming for validation. For love they never got.

I shut my eyes, taking a long sip of my coffee to bring me back to the coffee shop. I watched her adjust her blazer and shake her cup of coffee, lifting it to her pursed lips. The weight that hung on her almost made it uncomfortable to watch her eat, as if she felt so unworthy of life that it pained her to feed herself.

My heart wanted to cry out, "I don't *care*. I just want my mom!"

I had thought she might cry when I told her about my vision. That she'd deny everything, disappointed in me once again, and we'd figure out together why I would imagine such an awful thing. But this was worse. This made every seasick feeling, every nightmare, every nagging suspicion I'd had for the last fifteen years become a possible reality.

This felt like stepping out into space, only to realize I'd forgotten to tether myself to the ship.

Days after that conversation at the coffee shop, she'd apologize profusely over the phone, crying and saying she was relieved to have the truth out, but then within twenty four hours, she'd deny ever having that conversation. She was appalled that I could even *think* she'd do such a thing. It was exhausting and heartbreaking all over again, but I knew somewhere inside her, maybe now she'd start to forgive herself.

I nervously and very gently shared with Sam what our mom had confessed, hoping I could help bring her some closure as well, but she scoffed, interrupting me,

"Oh. I already *knew* that! She told me that years ago. Oh yeah, she knew the whole time it was happening."

Oh.

Ok…

She then nonchalantly let me know later, "Mom gave *me* all the court documents, but I already burned em, so, whatever you wanna know, I can just tell you."

"You *burned* em?"

It was all so much to digest at once, dropping down a whole other level, and Samantha was always waiting for me at the bottom, "Oh, you didn't *know*? That's too bad."

Shelby, a dear friend from work, sat with me at the outside cafe of Whole Foods, comparing notes and discussing similar struggles we were having. We'd become immediate friends, quoting Steel Magnolias and crackin' jokes in-between clients. People hustled around us oblivious, their carts full of overpriced produce and gluten free crackers while we sat there sobbing, and nodding to one another as we described the terrors we were uncovering.

These amazing women, who sat with me and cried, then cracked completely inappropriate jokes about the level of fucked up this had all reached... they saved me. They kept me from falling into the isolation tank of self-pity, of thinking no one else could possibly understand. She still texts me at the exact moments I need a friend, the very moments I need a good laugh. Even with a house full of wild boys running around her, she *always* knows. These are the angels that save us all when they don't even know it. The people who may not think of themselves as all that strong, when in reality, they've continued to get back up and love harder when most have given up on the world.

These are the sisters that come outta the wood work when our hearts are crying for family, for a hand to hold, throwing down a ladder so we can climb back out.

CHAPTER FIFTEEN

"Gonna open my heart right at the scar
and listen up."

Wait For Me

Kings of Leon

*M*om was ready to check herself into the
hospital, so we discussed it with Sam and decided to
take her together the following morning. I got to the
house around five that evening so I could make us some
supper and try to calm her nerves before bed. Hours
went by as mom and I sat on the couch, "Oh Rebecca. I
don't think I can do this anymore, I don't wanna do
this."

After the fifth call from Samantha, saying she
was on her way, she finally admitted she wasn't

coming. Mom started shaking worse as I hung up the phone, "She's not coming?"

"It's gonna be ok Mom, we're gonna do this together. Let's get you to bed so we can get some sleep." I needed to make myself a cup of tea and have a good cry before I turned in for the night, we had an exhausting day ahead of us.

Joe called soon after mom went to her room, "How ya doin' my babes?"

"Not real great. Mom's now changed her mind and is begging me not to take her, and of course Samantha planned all this, as usual, then decided *not* to come. So I'm just prayin' I don't have to physically put her in the car tomorrow morning."

He sighed, I could feel him shaking his head, "Of course she didn't... I'm so sorry babe."

He gave me one of his famous pep talks and let me cry it out, reminding me he had enough faith in me for the both of us, it would all be alright and he'd be waiting to hold me as soon as I got home.

I can do this. I, can do this.

I tapped on her bedroom door the next morning, slowly sliding it open to find her laying there wide awake.

"I never even slept Rebecca. Oh I'm just dreading this, I can't do this. Please don't make me go Rebecca!"

"*Yes* you can Mom, now come on let's get ready, what can I get you?"

"Oh Rebecca *please* don't do this!"

I marched around her four post bed like a cellblock warden. I turned on the shower for her, laid out her makeup and outfits, made some instant coffee she kept hidden out of sight from the missionaries, and went about my morning duties to keep my momentum.

She sat slumped in front of her vanity mirror. The bulbs around it buzzed as she curled her hair, laying the iron down next to her repeatedly to address my reflection,

"Oh Rebecca. Why am I even curling my hair, why do I even try at all? What have I done to my life Rebecca, your mommy's not even worth this makeup."

"You're doin' fine Mom, let's just get you ready ok."

I folded the blankets across her couch, wiped down the counters, and loaded my stuff into the car. When I walked back inside, she was standing at the window overlooking the golf course in her back yard, hugging a full change jar to her chest.

"Ooookay Mom, let's put the change jar down, we gotta get goin ok?"

"Rebecca! This is *all* I have!"

"Mom, you've got your wallet, I don't think you're gonna need a stash for the poker table while you're there," trying to make myself laugh, "you're only gonna be there as long as *you* want, so let's just put that away for now."

I peeled her fingers from the jar and quickly hid it from her sight before she could tackle me like a linebacker and run it to the back bedroom.

Thankfully I didn't have to physically lift her from the car when we got there, but I *did* know to quickly lock the doors as soon as I shut them. She reached for the handle, yanking it quickly and sighing, "Oh Rebecca… are you *sure* we have to do this?"

"You *asked* me to do this Mom, and I don't feel safe leavin' you home alone right now so we've *got* to try. Aaaaand here we go!"

I linked my arm with hers, kicking my heels like Willy Wonka. Partly out of playful distraction, and partly to gain momentum toward the entrance.

We got her checked in and into the back room when a wonderful nurse walked up to help her sort through her packed bag, looking for what she could keep and what would be locked up and returned when she checked out. She brought her a fresh toothbrush, soap, and booties. For some reason the shower essentials made the situation become a reality, and I started sobbing with exhaustion.

The mom I missed showed up for just a moment, "I know you're tired my Be. This has been a lot on you, I know. Mommy's alright now. You don't have to stay, they'll take care of the rest."

I hugged her and kissed her cheek, so proud of her again for doing what I knew she was afraid to do.

Forty eight hours later, I stood on the front porch of our apartment as she confessed over the phone that she'd been thinking about hurting her neighbor Ronda across the street. Justifying her plan with, "Rebecca, she's everything I'm not."

I had assumed the calls were monitored from inside the ward, and hoping she was being at least somewhat honest with her doctors. But they weren't, and she wasn't. She left to return home that very afternoon, when Sam came to her rescue.

I spent every day just trembling with anxiety, waiting for a phone call from the police. I called a place I knew she was attending group counseling.

"Hey so, listen, I know how H.I.P.P.A violations work and what not, so, I'm just gonna talk, and you chime in at any moment. Please."

The woman listened to me on the other end, and answered me after a long sigh, "Honey… I wish I had something better to tell you, but *until* she hurts someone or herself, there's nothing we can do. You can have her held for up to 24 hours, but if she shows no sign of a threat, they have to release her. I'm so sorry."

The woman gave me the number for an emergency unit I could call and I thanked her for being honest with me.

Mom had decided not to answer her phone for days at a time, letting us think she'd killed herself, only to call us back at the last minute, asking why we were so worried. "I've been right here the whole time," she'd say.

I made a call to her neighbor across the street, the one she'd been obsessing over for the last year and was evidently making plans about. I left her as subtle a voice message as I could,

"Hey Miss Ronda, this is Becca, Beverly's daughter? Yeah um, I just wanted to letcha know, she's been going through some rough stuff lately and it would *really* be best if you maybe kept a little space from her for a while. I really appreciate you keeping an eye on her for us, she just needs a little time."

Sam thought I was overreacting.

I mean, I wasn't gonna tell Ronda,

"Hey you should probably lock your doors cause my mom's been planning some single white female shit." But I *had* to say *something*!

All I kept imagining was what I'd have to say to Ronda's children, grandchildren, and family when they asked why no one said anything. Why no one was keeping an eye on *their* mom.

I'd been mentally preparing for losing my own mom to suicide for years, but the thought of having to apologize to someone else for losing their's because of mine? I couldn't even imagine.

I finally received a call from Mom the following evening, she let me know she'd been across the street at Ronda's for a steak dinner. She'd probably heard the damn voice mail when I left it.

Oh yeah, *great* idea. Invite her for steak, just hand her a serrated knife…

My nerves were officially shot.

We never want to imagine that evil exists intertwined with our ever day lives, weaved throughout our best intentions. That the very people we exhaust

245

ourselves trying to save, may be the ones who want to see us dead. It's not real comforting realizing it's not that easy to draw a straight line down the middle of good and evil, to spot the fly in the ointment without hesitation. It's not something to lose our minds focusing on daily by any means, but this darkness hiding in plain sight has made itself known to me so many times throughout my life, I can't deny the drive I feel to call it out. To demand it show itself and retract its need to manipulate and torture the ones I love.

I remember there was a week around Christmas, I was maybe twelve, that *every time* one of us walked through the living room, we'd wrinkle our noses,

"What IS that!?"

There was this awful, sweet smell permeating the room, and the heat from the fireplace made it even thicker and nauseating.

A few days after the smell finally started to dissipate, my dad walked into the kitchen as mom stood stirring dinner on the stove. He was holding the handle to a plastic bucket he'd found tucked in the corner of the living room behind a large reading chair. The bottom was completely melted out.

"Beverly. Did you put hot coals from the woodstove in this bucket?"

246

Her face had no expression. She panned her eyes to the bucket, and then back to him, "Yes."

"…Beverly, why the *hell* would you put hot coals, in a *plastic* ice cream bucket!? And then set it on the *carpet*!? Beverly, it burned a hole clear through the padding… There ain't nothin' but a charred circle left! You bout burned the whole house down!"

"Daniel! How was I supposed to know that!? I was just *trying* to clean up! But I guess I can't do *anything* right can I?"

Pointing furiously at the tall metal bucket and shovel sitting on the brick next to the wood stove, he yelled, "The bucket's *right there*! We've used it this whole time! For five years!! You knew that!"

"Well I'm sorry I can't do anything right! That's *all* I ever hear," now mocking herself, impersonating her own mother's voice, "Beverly doesn't have enough sense to pour it out of a boot…"

I walked in the living room to examine the area. He wasn't kidding. There was a perfect black charred circle burned into the plywood.

I never really thought about the reality of the situation at the time. That we were *extremely* lucky our house hadn't gone up in flames, or that she knew exactly what she was doing. She's *not* dumb, and neither is my dad, but they've both always been extremely talented at appearing oblivious to the most obvious things, particularly when they need to dodge the truth.

CHAPTER SIXTEEN

"Oh come on be alive again, don't lay
down and die."

Malibu

Hole

I'd finally cut ties with Kumu and the healing
group before we'd moved into our new studio
apartment. She'd had me on the phone every other day
now, sometimes for three or four hours. I knew she was
isolating me from Joe, and I didn't like what I saw
happening behind the scenes. I got the courage to call
her and turn down the teaching position with her in
Kauai. I told her I'd pay back whatever the ticket cost
was, but I knew this wasn't for me at that time in my
life.

She got extremely sharp with me, telling me I
was afraid and making a huge mistake.

"I'm not a gambling woman," she said, "but I'll bet you won't last three months without us!"

I told her to go ahead 'n place that bet, and I hung up the phone.

I had enough to juggle, I didn't need to exhaust myself bein' the personal assistant and second in command to a self-professed spiritual master.

I'd revisit that relationship years later to end it for good.

My health was becoming unavoidably worse, but I didn't have the time or mental capacity to worry about that right now. I applied canker sore medicine to the inside of my bottom lip every morning, chugged apple cider vinegar, and just told myself it'd get better once things with our mom cooled down.

Taking the first sip of my Corona one afternoon, I turned to a friend of ours,

"Hey do you like, ever get this warm tight feeling in your muscles after your first sip of beer?"

"You mean, like a buzz?"

"No I mean, like, your *very* first sip."

"Mmm, no?"

Yeah me neither…

It was so embarrassing, some days I felt too inebriated to drive after having *half* a beer, and I was a six Guinness kinda girl y'all. I'd sit and order food waiting for it to go away, but meanwhile my limbs were filling with lead the longer I sat.

My hands started feeling heavy and disconnected. I was struggling just to fill out the medical intake forms at work. My arms started darting and shaking the harder I tried to hold them still, tossing and spilling things constantly. I was staying nauseous throughout the day and getting light headed in the middle of massages, checking the time and thinking, "I can do this, just three more hours."

I walked out of a session to grab water for my client and I remember rubbing my hand along the left side of my neck, swallowing and thinking, "Oh geez I hope my other tonsil's not gettin' infected now…" I could feel a tiny lump everytime I swallowed.

The nights I forced myself to go out, I struggled to even pay attention during conversation. I was too busy focusing on my sore throat and burning eyes.

Dusti has a severe corn allergy, and you can probably guess how easily and often she accidentally got dosed, so we ended up spending a lot of weekends taking it easy, recouping and drinking tea on the porch.

I was so connected to my mother's mental state, like a flashing baby monitor, I'd feel it the moment she

251

took a nose dive. I'd send her texts when I felt her dipping again, and she'd answer me back,

"Is the bad stuff around?"

I'd never talked to her about sensing or feeling anything bad, spirits or entities or anything like that, but for some reason overnight, that's how she started addressing it when she wasn't doing well, as if we'd regularly discussed dark forces.

She kept the radio in her living room on the Christian station, just loud enough to hear it humming in the background all day. We'd never even vaguely discussed what she was trying to protect herself from.

The bells on the doors, the sage bundles she always kept around the house. She'd roll her eyes addressing my sensitive and intuitive nature, saying that I should be going to church as she was, but I think she was *really* just like me.

When I was staying in Pennsylvania, her Aunt Wilma would sit downstairs in the living room belting out, "Hooooooome, hooooome on the raaaaange!" Her preacher had suggested she sing it to keep the demons away.

I mean, I would've maybe thought something slightly more, hymn-ish? But hey, maybe cowboy campfire songs are the untapped Achilles heel of evil.

Either way, this feeling of being hounded by spirits had *obviously* not started with my mother.

I always knew the days she was feeling bombarded and exhausted, because my body felt like someone pulled my plug from its socket.

A new couple, Rick and Lindsay, had moved in next door to us, and I immediately got a bad vibe from the woman. Bad enough I gifted her one of my motorcycle helmets. After seeing her boyfriend rode a Harley as well, I presented her with an olive branch. I felt her watching me, competing and scheming, and all I could think was, "Bitch, I *beg* of you, please take your mess somewhere else."

It's a small world, and Joe had met the guy she was dating years before while he was still bartending. We decided the four of us should take a ride to South Port for lunch the following Saturday. Again, like always, I was hoping she'd prove my suspicions wrong, but those gut feelings usually end up correct.

It was a warm day, but I zipped up my long sleeve leather jacket, jeans and Doc Martens. I then heard, "Bring a couple Band-Aids."

Joe came down the stairs with his vest on, "Ya don't think you're gonna get hot in that jacket babe? It's pretty warm."

"Nah, you know how I am." Sliding two Band-Aids into my breast pocket.

"What's with the Band-Aids?"

"I dunno," I shrugged, "they said to bring em."

He just smiled and handed me my helmet, locking the door behind us.

We were coming down Carolina Beach Road with our neighbors riding behind us. I was looking at the used cars in the lot next us thinking, "I wonder if I'd know what to do in an accident, if I'd react quickly…"

I found out about 3 minutes later.

Joe locked up the brakes as I screamed, "Babe RED LIGHT!" The bike started fishtailing and I came off the back doing a soft ball slide and hit my feet running toward him as the bike rolled over on itself, flattening the handle bars to the gas tank. I was picking up pieces from the headlight and turn signals running through the intersection. All the cars came to a complete stop just watching us. When I got to him, he was laying on his back after kicking bike to keep it from rolling on top of him. We were stunned but knew we had to get outta the intersection quickly. He picked the bike up to push it into the gas station, as I ran to the median where our neighbors were standing, white as ghosts.

254

"I don't know how y'all even moved that fast," Rick said, "I didn't even have my kickstand down and y'all were already on your feet."

I had my arms wrapped around Lindsay trying to calm her down, she was more freaked out than I was. I'm sure we were quite the sight with Joe catapulting from his bike and me running at him in my Evel Knievel helmet. #dressedfortheoccassion

"We're ok," I kept telling her, "we're alright, it's ok."

We crossed the street to the gas station and Rick went inside to buy us a pack of cigarettes. Who should pull up in the parking lot as we stood there, but Jay.

"Hey are y'all alright!? What the fuck happened? Did y'all just get in an accident?!"

We lit our cigarettes, filling Jay in on our attempted but *not* so graceful stunt, and I pulled the two Band-Aids from my pocket, one for the scrape on Joe's palm and the other for the road rash on his arm.

The sleeve on my jacket took all the road rash, and I surprisingly didn't have a scratch. My angels were right again.

Now, I would've thought, that that experience would defuse some of the anger or whatever it was this woman Lindsay felt toward me, bond us a little… but it did *not*.

During tea time with Dusti a couple weeks later, I got a flash across my mind of my blue and white flower pot being smashed, just so she could watch me pick up the pieces from her downstairs window.

A week later, as Joe and I came up the stairs to our front door, there were pieces of blue and white ceramic scattered across the porch, my poor lil pot. I rolled my eyes and shook my head, "Saw that one comin'…"

Not getting enough of a reaction from the broken pot evidently, Lindsay made up an outlandish story, that Joe and I had an explosive argument nights before, and she almost called the cops for fear it would turn physical.

The thing about these kinda people, is that they're often not smart enough to realize how horrible their lying is. These were some *cheap* studio apartments, you could hear your neighbor's tinder alerts dinging in the middle of the night, so… an explosive argument? Trust me, we *all* would've heard it.

I just ignored her and went about my business, but that only worked for a few days until she had Rick contact Joe, asking him why I was being so hateful to his girlfriend.

I'd fuckin' had it by that point. I got home that afternoon and Joe and I both asked Rick to tell his girlfriend to please find another hobby. I then approached her myself the next morning as she was leaving for work.

"Ok Lindsay, what is the deal, have I done something to upset you?"

"No!" She said, acting surprised and clueless.

Beeeeetch please.

"Alright well here's the deal, I got enough shit goin' on. I don't know *who* you supposedly heard fighting, or how we *all* managed to miss it *except for you*, but I'd appreciate you keep the stories to yourself."

She grit her teeth, forcing a painful smile, and left for work in her own little fit of fury. That afternoon, I was on the porch journaling when she got home. She walked past me silently, and as she stuck her keys into the lock, I watched a black dripping tar figure follow her right through the front door.

Just like the things I'd felt and seen around my own mother.

Here's the truth Empaths- We can do everything humanly possible to assure someone we are in no competition, we don't want any trouble, we'd like to be friends, but that's just *not* the kinda company they keep. They're *used* to being followed by sticky situations, that's where they thrive. All we can really do is separate ourselves from people like that.

Sometimes it's easier to see these toxic traits in strangers and asshole neighbors though ain't it? When it's people we love or look up to. We've usually been making excuses for them for a long time already, so their malignant nature *is* the norm. Those panic alerts and red flags don't stand out as much anymore. That's when it gets a little more complicated to navigate. Something absolutely outlandish has to happen for us to say,

"Whoa now, hold on just a minute! I don't deserve that!"

CHAPTER SEVENTEEN

"Somethin' happened along the way,
what used to be happy was sad."

After The Love Has Gone

Earth, Wind & Fire

"I just don't understand *why* you need to be there Rebecca!" It had taken five phone calls for me to get the date and time of my mother's next doctor's appointment. I wanted to be there for her assessment while he adjusted her medication, to see how much of the truth she was really telling.

"I just wanna make sure he's listening to you and putting you on the correct dosages Mom. I'm not even gonna say a word unless something's overlooked."

She was *not* happy with me coming, but she wasn't changing my mind.

Our shoes clunked down the sterile hallway as Dr. Gregory walked out to greet us, covering his apprehension with a painted on smile.

"So good to see you Beverly, come on back."

My mother had become frightening to sit in a room with. Family members didn't like having her in their homes anymore, and asked that I only visit with her in public places from now on.

"Alright Bev, so I know it's been a little while since our last visit, so I'll just remind you to listen to each question, and just answer as best you can with how you've been feeling the last couple weeks alright? We wanna make sure we adjust any dosages or medications correctly."

"Yes doctor Gregory," she whimpered.

They breezed through the list until, "Any suicidal thoughts or tendencies?"

"No."

Objection! I sat forward to address her.

"Mom...?"

Her head turned to me with an awful jerk and I sat straight up in my seat.

"Mom, you *have* had suicidal *and* homicidal thoughts, a lot lately."

She stared at me in complete silence and animosity. I waited to hear the legs of her chair squeak when she lunged to wrap her hands around my throat.

"Beverly?" Dr. Gregory said quietly, "Is this true?"

She didn't acknowledge him. Anyone who's experienced this look, knows why it's called, "Shark Eyes." When someone's eyes become void of any life, and your stomach drops twelve floors when they look at you. It's paralyzing.

I broke from the trance and turned to face the doctor,

"She's been talking about suicide for months now, but during her recent stay at the hospital, she confessed she's also been thinking about hurting her neighbor across the street."

"Ok, so you *have* been having suicidal and homicidal thoughts for some time now Beverly, is that correct?"

She finally blinked, but only turned to face him and then back at me, making a clicking noise against her bottom teeth.

He took that as a yes, made note of it, nervously adjusted his glasses, and continued scrolling through the questionnaire.

Lucky him, he didn't have to ride home with her.

I did my best the following weeks to keep myself focused on work, and the trip Joe and I had planned for my upcoming birthday. We decided it'd be a good idea to go stay in the mountains for a few days, we could both use some peace and quiet.

Dusti and I sat at our booth by the window at our usual brunch spot, sipping coffee and polishing off our plates. We had one more refill on our coffees so she could laugh and snort her way through her latest date play by play. She always had good stories to fill me in on for our brunch dates, so it usually took at least six cups of coffee for us to get each other caught up.

My cell phone rang as I buckled my seat belt and we started toward home, "Hey babe! We're just headin' your way!"

"Hey my love, it's cool no rush um… I was callin' ya cause I just got off the phone with Liam. I just, I just found out Chachi was in an accident last night."

"Oh no! Do you want us to meet you at the hospital or-"

"He didn't make it babe."

This man was a true character. His fingers were curled and crooked from years of boxing, and he was one of those people that hollered and hand gestured to communicate as much as he used his scratchy Chicago accent to form words. He couldn't get outta the parking garage next to the bar he owned one night, so he got out of his car, ripped the arm off, and went on his merry way. I showed up to his bar one night, sunburnt and exhausted, just stopping by to see Joe at work, and he slid a shot glass up to me, pouring he and I a shot of Rumple Minz,

"Ahhhhh! Every lobsta deserves a shot!" he hollered. He clinked his glass with mine, threw it back and, poured us another one. He never slowed down. Losing him was a hard hit for a lot of people in Wilmington.

I stood in front of the mirror, applying makeup in our upstairs bathroom three days before his funeral. I was thinking about Joe and I's upcoming trip, and whether we should take the bike with all the rain we'd been having.

This persistent beeping started coming from somewhere in the house. I stopped, looked over the banister, but heard nothing else, so I went back to the mirror. Then it started again. I looked at the smoke detector, but it was fine. Then the beeping became faster.

"Oh what the fuck is this." I thought. I slapped my mascara down on the counter and started down the stairs, following the sound, not sure what I was about to walk up on.

I came around the corner and into our kitchen to find the beeping was coming from the microwave. Numbers flashed across the screen as if someone was punching a calculator.

Naturally I began punching numbers right back, as if *that* would fix it. I somehow managed to lock the microwave and it started flashing, "Power level may not be changed at this time."

I turned and looked around me, "Hello?" Maybe a poltergeist just needed some help nuking their Hot Pocket. I mean, I got you ghosty, I know the struggle.

I paused, waiting for an answer, and then turned to put some plates away in the cabinet when there stood Chachi, jumping up and down emphatically, "Ahhhhh I know you can hear me you crazy bitch!"

I froze, watching him out of the left corner of my vision. He was laughing and kicking his legs up like a little kid, so excited he'd finally gotten my attention.

He fumbled over his words, wanting Joe to know he was truly a brother to him, and how much he loved him.

Then the next day, Joe turned his radio down over and over on his way home, hearing a Harley riding next to him, but checking his mirrors to see no one. He must've been making a lot of rounds to visit everyone before his funeral.

Most of us had spent the night out before the service. I drank water and taxied Joe around to see his guys, sharing stories and grieving into the early morning. One of the regular patrons and friends went into a seizure shortly after the first procession. Everyone held onto him and cried waiting for the ambulance. It was just an unbearable day for a lot of people.

Joe and I got home to the apartment after the burial, completely drained and just ready to lay down before the celebration of life planned that evening. I took our pup Dilly out for a walk and returned Mom's call I'd missed earlier that morning.

"Hey Mom, sorry I missed ya earlier, it's been a really *really* long day with the funeral 'n everything. We just now got home to walk Dilly and lay down for a minute."

"Oh Rebecca, I've been waitin' for you to call me back all mornin'. I need you to come up and take me back to the hospital."

"Today? You mean right *now*?"

"Yes Rebecca, I've been sitting here with the phone next to me since eight this mornin."

"Mom, I seriously *cannot* do it today. Sam's forty minutes from you, why don't you-"

"Oh Rebecca…"

"Mom, look. We've been crying for the last forty-eight hours straight. We *might've* slept two hours last night, just finished putting Joe's friend in an ambulance, then attended the grave side, and just now have a second to rest. I am exhausted. This was one of Joe's best friends. I am not leaving him today."

"But Rebecca I'm your MOTHER!"

"Joe needs me to today. I can take you first thing tomorrow morning, but today Joe needs me. You can call Samantha."

And with that, she hung up on me.

I turned on my heels, swinging the plastic bag of Dilly's fresh turd like Fred Astaire's umbrella. "What a fuckin' day huh?" Dilly just squinted at the sun, blinking her little white eye lashes at me.

Nothing, absolutely *nothing,* was ever going to stop my mother from sabotaging every moment of my life. Whether good or bad, if she wasn't clearly the first priority, she *had* to interfere. It was never gonna stop, and I couldn't take it anymore. Not unless the next time I drove her to the hospital I just went ahead and booked a room for two.

CHAPTER EIGHTEEN

"And I got nothin' to lose but darkness
and shadows. Got nothin' to lose but bitterness
and patterns."

Got Nuffin

Spoon

I opened the coffee maker in our little mountain cabin to find a diamond ring, and Joe sat behind me smiling ear to ear, peering over a pillow he was hugging to his chest.

"Is this…is this for ME!?" I squealed. At first thinking the previous vacationers had possibly forgotten jewelry. I'm not real good with subtle hints sometimes, at least of the romantic kind.

It wasn't even a question if I should marry him. He felt more like home than anything I'd ever felt. He made me feel at home in myself, and he never looked away when I showed the worst sides of myself. He taught me what unconditional love actually is.

I couldn't stop looking at the diamond on my hand while I drove us home from our much needed getaway.

"You know I can't have like, a *wedding* wedding right? My nerves just can't handle it. I mean I can't even regularly handle celebratin' my own birthday."

I also knew, it was time to cut communication with my mom. I just wanted to be able to breath, to enjoy being happy without waiting for the phone to ring every second of the day. I knew there was no way I could have her attend our wedding without having a complete nervous breakdown.

Even though I had spent much of our weekend in the bathroom or taking another dose of probiotics, I still didn't realize how fragile my health had gotten. I was just surviving at that point, ignoring the fact I couldn't go ten minutes without gritting my teeth or hiding the tears welling up. I tried to stay as stoic about cutting ties with my mom as possible, "It's just what has to be done," I told myself. "It'll be fine. You'll be fine."

Joe never stated his opinion on either side of the matter, he just rode with me to the restaurant to meet her. He sat next to me, holding my hand under the table. Sam was supposed to be there with us, agreeing for months she also couldn't take it anymore, but she'd called on our way there to say she wouldn't be coming and to leave her out of it. So I did.

I took long deep breaths, squeezing Joes hand and trying not to watch Mom's shoulders shaking under her blazer. The waitress interrupted quietly and I tried to smile, signaling it wasn't a good time for dessert orders.

"Mom, I'm gonna end up in the hospital myself, I can't do this anymore. Until you start helping yourself, I have nothing left to give. We've been having the same conversations for over thirteen years. I deserve to be healthy and happy, and right now I'm afraid I won't even be able to have babies of my own, my body's just too exhausted."

She didn't respond much except to ask what Samantha through about all this, and I informed her that the decision to cut contact was mine alone, and Sam had nothing to do with it.

I drove her car home from the restaurant while Joe followed behind us. I didn't want her driving, I was

271

afraid she might get in an accident she was in such a daze. She reached for my hand looking out the window and biting on her toothpick, but never spoke.

I climbed in the passenger seat next to Joe after getting her home, and she just stood there in the driveway watching us. He started backing down the driveway and she ran toward the car, sliding her hands down my window, "Rebecca please don't do this!"

I sobbed, "Babe just go, please just go." Trying to keep my eyes straight ahead while she followed us down the driveway.

I cried and cried the entire ride home, begging my angels quietly to help me release the guilt when she hurts herself or someone else, to hold me and remind me I'd done everything I could. I felt them comforting me, and Joe squeeze onto my hand.

"Why have I had to feel *so much* incredible pain my entire life?" I pleaded.

"So that you may sing it for others when they can't yet find the words." they responded.

"Then it's gonna be ok," I thought, "then it's worth it. I can do that."

It's gonna be ok.

I kissed Joes hand and took a deep breath, letting the pain subside and looking at the road ahead.

All heart break is awful, but there's a different kind of pain when you voluntarily step into the bear trap. When it's not only the weight of loss that snaps you in two, but guilt, waves of remorse and grief. When we abruptly cut ties with someone we love because they're killing us, it doesn't feel like a victory. It feels like survival. Losing a limb to free ourselves. It's a last resort, but we're not ready to give up on our life. Not yet.

Every time I'd cried for the last ten years, all I could say over and over to vocalize my pain was, "I'm tired. I'm just so tired."

Leaving her home as she stood in the driveway, I started to see why I'd been tired for *so* long. Why I could never seem to catch a breath, but now, maybe that would change. The helpless child in me that had been impatiently waiting her execution, was standing up to hold hands with the woman now planning their escape. I knew that walking away might actually kill my mom, but for the first time in my life, I chose to save myself.

The next year wasn't easy, and I continuously reminded family and friends to please not mention our wedding to my mom, and as our day approached, the wedding itself seemed to be more and more of a burden on my family.

273

I think I cried the whole week before our wedding.

I hadn't invited but a few friends and family for our simple ceremony. I wanted to keep things as small as possible and I didn't wanna put anybody out. Sam had volunteered to take pictures, but was now calling to say she was so sick from her recent pregnancy, she wasn't sure if she'd even make it. I tried to accommodate her,

"I'll bring you ginger tea and have 'em make you a special meal that sounds good to you! Whatever you wa-"

"Yeah no. I'm still gonna wanna vomit every ten minutes. It's whatever. I'll try and be there but, I can't promise I won't have to leave." she grumbled.

The phone rang shortly after I hung up with her and it was Ronda, my mom's neighbor,

"Hey Rebecca, I was just calling to let you know that your mom's checked herself back into the hospital. She just wanted me to let you know."

"It's just as well," I thought, "at least she's somewhere safe." Not seeing it at the time as another sabotage, but somebody had obviously been talking to mom about the wedding.

We'd booked our flights to leave for Ireland two days after the ceremony, and by that point, I just wanted to get on the plane and never come back. If it hadn't been for Christa showing up and holding my hand, I don't know if I'd have made it through our wedding day. I was a *mess* y'all. A hot hot mess.

Dad and Janice stayed at a relative's house nearby with my sister, her husband, and their kids. I called his cell phone the morning of the ceremony, excited they'd come and were gonna join us for breakfast.

"Hey Dad!"

"Heeeey it's the bride!"

"Dad I'm so excited! What time do y'all wanna do breakfast!?"

"Weeeeeell, lemme ask Samantha and see how she's feelin'. She may not be up for it, we may just snack on somethin' here."

I tried to hide the fact that my voice was starting to shake. This was the one day I wanted my family to show up and be excited with me, and I still just felt like this entire thing was another burden to them.

Joe was getting dressed and I turned my head so he couldn't see my eyes getting red. My dad hollered up the stairs to my sister and then spoke back into the phone,

"How bout uhh… how bout I call ya back in a lil bit. She's sayin' she didn't sleep too good and needs a minute to see how she's feelin'."

I swallowed the lump in my throat, "Yeah that's, that's fine. We'll just um, I mean, yeah if you change your mind I mean we could just go somewhere near y'all so you only have to drive like five minutes. We'll just wait for a lil while." I had girls coming to do my hair and makeup scheduled, but I didn't want them to feel rushed.

I mean it wasn't her fault she had morning sickness, but I couldn't help wanting to cry. Her wedding had been a weekend production. Dad had called in for shaved ice machines at the last minute, frantic to make everything perfect! Mom was running in circles setting up tables and screaming about who was gonna pick up Dusty Miller.

"Who the *hell's* Dusty Miller!?" I kept yelling, lugging white lights and ribbons out of the trunk. I guess she thought I was just bein' a smartass, cause she wouldn't answer me for a good hour until she went into hysterics.

Ohhhhh, Dusty Miller is a *plant*! And in fact it was *me* who was sent to go pick it up. Well, glad I found out who it was. Could've gotten that done a *lot* sooner had I known it wasn't a random priesthood holder I was supposed to remember from church.

We made it through breakfast fine, and I managed to not cry into my sausage and gravy biscuits, (Jesus took that wheel.) but Christa knew as soon as we got out to the parking lot, I needed champagne. Badly. She immediately turned to me smiling, "Mimosas?"

My girl.

The rest of the day, couldn't have gone better. A friend came to do my hair and makeup, while another friend of Joe's that managed a riverfront restaurant, reserved the outdoor area for us free of charge. Jay even agreed to officiate. It was perfect. We wrote our own vows and got to cry and laugh through the whole thing. We had a short quick ceremony before appetizers arrived, and that was it! Then we could just enjoy the rest of the evening with our friends and family. Stress, over. We ended the night at Mugsy's Pub, dancing barefoot to the jukebox and eating chicken tenders. I was a happy girl.

We flew out for our honeymoon in Ireland two days later, staying in a hotel across from the train

277

station in Dublin. We got up every morning to walk the city, watching the shops open and pub owners unlock their doors. We felt like we were in our own little world for that week.

We toured the Wicklow Mountains and I'll never forget the light in Joe's eyes, watching the sheep running through the heather on the countryside. We took pictures sitting on the bridge used for *P.S. I Love You*, and stood there holding onto each other. We'd both come a long way since that night at Drifter's. We strolled through markets, putting on hats and gorgeous wool coats, laughing like little kids, "Try this one! Try this one!" The weather was so gorgeous while we were there, the first week of school was pushed back for all the children so they could enjoy the warm Mediterranean days.

We climbed into bed the second to last night of our honeymoon, and set the alarm for an early train ride to Haute, a seaside town not far away. I think we were just as excited about the train ride as we were the town itself. Around midnight, I was jolted awake with a heavy hit to the pit of my stomach. I sat up, nauseous and uneasy, looking around the room. A sinister energy sank across the bed and I stared at the mirrors along the sliding closet doors.

Joe sat up a few seconds later, "What's going on?"

"I dunno," I said trembling, "I was dead asleep and woke up feeling this awful like evil presence before I even opened my eyes…"

He pulled me closer and we both took a few long looks around the room before laying our heads back down. I listened to his breathing become slow and steady again as he fell back to sleep, and I laid there and prayed. Something was *really* wrong, I didn't know what, but I couldn't shake it. I felt my guardians sit around us and hold onto me,

"You're on your honeymoon Rebecca, just be happy. It's <u>ok</u> to be happy, you deserve to be happy."

My heart rate finally began to calm, and I tucked my head back into Joe's chest and fell asleep.

We got our coffee and made it on the early morning train. The sun washed over rows of old chimneys and weathered brick factories along the train tracks, as the rhythmic thumping and clanking rocked us back and forth. We winked at one another over our coffee cups, keeping quiet while everyone around us read the morning paper and straightened their ties and socks.

After finding a small cafe for breakfast, we followed a steep cobblestone road uphill, peaking in store windows and listening to the seals barking and splashing behind a tug boat idling out to the open water. The smell of the docks, diesel fuel, and fishing nets felt like home. No matter where I've been in the world, certain smells, certain people, certain routines still stay the same, still remind me I'm exactly the same person I was ten thousand miles before.

I was on my honeymoon, married, across the Atlantic, and still trying to analyze this too familiar sinking in my gut that wouldn't seem to leave. Again I heard, "Rebecca, you *deserve* to be happy. It's ok to be happy."

The next evening, we were seated next to each other laughing and recounting our adventures as the plane touched down in Boston. We'd spent the entire flight stealing kisses and squeezing one another's hand. Two girls sitting behind us tapped our shoulders as the plane landed and the cabin lights came on, "We're not trying to be creepy or anything, but seriously, we hope we can have a relationship like that someday. You guys are really lucky."

I promise, there's *never* been a day since we started dating, that we haven't said to one another, "We are so lucky." Everyone needs someone they can hold onto.

The aisle filled as everyone stood to grab their suitcases from the overhead compartments and phones dinged and flashed as everyone's text messages and voicemails flooded in. We sat patiently, in no hurry to be done with our honeymoon, and I reached for my phone at the bottom of my carry-on.

We discussed where we might want to eat before our next flight into Raleigh, and my heart stopped as the screen on my phone lit up with missed messages. An unknown number at the top read,

"Good Evening, this is the East ***** Police Department. Please respond directly to this text message as soon possible or by calling this number-"

Joe watched my face go pale, and I tilted the screen so he could read the message. He just looked back at me speechless, holding tighter to my hand. Everyone around us unwrapped protein bars, and zippers flew shut as the line began to move and people made their way off the plane.

I was shaking, trying to remind myself not to take shallow breaths, I could feel the blood trying to come back to my face with every slow inhale. There was only one reason that the Police Department would be contacting me, either my mom was dead, or she'd killed someone else.

We sat motionless, looking at each other, breathing in and out in unison. I pushed the power button on my phone, tucked it back into the bottom of my bag, and smiled at him, "We're still on our honeymoon."

I knew I had to keep my shit together for us to get on our connecting flight. They're not huge about hysteria in airports, I get it. We got ourselves some food and I picked at my plate of fries, texting both my dad and sister saying, "Hey we made it into Boston, I know something's happened with mom but I wanna wait to talk about it until we've made it to Raleigh. I need to *not* become a blubbering mess for at least another three hours, I'll call you then."

Walking through the parking deck, loaded down with our bags, I promised Joe ten times that I was fine to drive the two hours home.

When I'm under severe stress, I tend to get *extra* Stuart from Mad TV, "Staaahhhp! I can do it myself!"

We got about ten minutes down the road, and after no response from either text, I called Sam, but she replied in her usual cold nonchalant tone,

"It's not for you to worry about, I already handled it."

"Samantha. You're not even gonna tell me what happened?! So you're not even gonna tell me if Mom's *alive*…"

"Rebecca, you're on your honeymoon, I get it, I took care of everything already. I don't see how you *knowing* anything is gonna help."

I became hysterical.

"Samantha she's MY MOM TOO! I got a text from the Police Department so OBVIOUSLY there's something I should know about! Why can't you just tell me!?"

"Rebecca…"

"I'm not gonna ask you again. This is ridiculous."

"Alright, fine. Mom tried to kill herself. She took a full bottle of her pills, but she's stable, some ladies from church found her in time."

By this point I'd turned my hazards on and was pulling the car to the side of the road so Joe could drive. Sam recounted what had transpired, that she'd picked up the pieces while I was busy on my honeymoon.

All I could think about was the women that had to find our mom. They *never* should have had to

283

witness that, images they'll never get out of their minds. They were scheduled to come visit her at six that evening, the same time Joe and I had sat up in our hotel room over three thousand miles across the Atlantic. Mom had taped a note to her front door that read, "Call the funeral home." If it hadn't been for them, she wouldn't have made it.

We got home and got back to work, and I struggled not to let my eyes droop when coworkers and clients asked about our honeymoon. It had been absolutely wonderful, we were beside ourselves walking around Dublin without a plan or care in the world, and then as soon as we made it back, that feeling had been snatched away from us the second our plane landed. I felt angry. Cheated and exhausted.

I was so ecstatically happy, but I'd had to fight tooth and nail for every bit of it. I had to argue my right to it every day, and I was becoming infuriated that not even my wedding day, not even my honeymoon, could be left alone, untainted without guilt and shame.

Not surprisingly, Sam's nausea had even completely cleared up just in time to put on a good face for everyone attending our wedding. Funny how that happens.

The only way I'd ever known how to try and rid myself of the heavy pangs of guilt, was to hold tighter to my family, to try and make up for everything. To try and please them even harder.

I missed my aunt Val and Grandma Sheryl at our wedding, but completely understood they couldn't travel. I wanted to get up to visit soon after we got back from our honeymoon. Our Gammaw (we always called her) had been battling cancer for some time, she'd lost her sweetheart and we knew she was tired. I wanted to make it home so bad to visit her and hold her hand, but every time we got ready to make the trip, I felt like I was coming down with strep throat, and I didn't want to bring that around her, so we'd postpone the drive once again.

I laid awake in bed one night and prayed to her, seeing myself wrapping my arms around her petite little frame and kissing her forehead. I wanted her to feel peace and I assured her,

"Gammaw if you're scared, I'll come with you. When you're ready to go just come tap me and I'll be there."

I dreamt that night that I walked into her and Granddaddy's home, and she ran to me from the living room, swinging her arms in excitement, "Oh I'm so

285

glad you're here! No one else will come back here with me!"

She stood to my chest, squeezing me tightly as she always had, and held onto my hand, leading me down the long hallway into their bedroom. To the left of the doorway was her mother, sleeping soundly on a marble slab wrapped in beautiful silk shawls. Two girls stood by her side smiling sweetly and watching over her. They looked to be sisters around ages nine and six, and I gathered they weren't saying anything because they spoke Spanish. Knowing their words would be lost on us, they stayed silent, but their sweet spirits were palpable. I woke up shortly after this thinking, "Well that was… different."

Joe and I finally made it up to see her the following weekend. I sat next to her, hugging her little knees to my side. We showed her pictures from our honeymoon, describing our wedding and the Wicklow Mountains. My aunt Val had never left her side for months now, watching NCIS for days on end and being her around the clock caretaker.

Grandma's right eye was closed now, but she still held her left open to look at us. She leaned forward to me when there was a pause in the conversation, and tapped her index finger lightly against my forehead,

"When you're ready," she said quietly, "I'll come get you."

Tears welled up as we all started laughing, "I have no doubt you will Gammaw."

She'd heard me.

I love her so, I still feel her telling me to just go for it whenever I'm afraid, twisting her hips in the kitchen and playing that Ray Stevens record.

The hair on my head stood up, recalling my dream when Aunt Val told us later that Grandma would *not* stop talking about how quiet the twins were.

"Those twins don't talk much do they,"Grandma had kept saying.

Aunt Val, understandably assuming she was referring to my sister's kids, responded over and over, "Mama, you didn't talk to the twins today, remember?"

When she passed, I'd driven up for one more visit. I got to sit with her one more time, giggle with her and feel her warm hand on my cheek when she smiled and called me, "sweet baby." I was about to leave the house and drive back when I got the call that she was gone. I went to shut the bathroom door behind me and heard two quick knocks. I laughed and started to cry, I knew she was more than alright. I was also sure Granddaddy greeted her like he always used to do when she was pulling sweet potato biscuits outta the oven, "Mmm mm mmm girl. Shaped like a Coca-Cola bottle."

When we lost our Gammaw, something changed. The thread running through our entire family seemed to be cut loose, it felt like when she'd crossed the veil, another had been lifted.

I wonder if this isn't how many family's come face to face with their healing, when someone who's held everyone together for so long is no longer there to do it. Everyone turns to face one another like, "Now what?"

CHAPTER NINETEEN

"It's been a long long war, now the
battle's drawing near."

Tiny Light

Grace Potter & The Nocturnals

"I mean look at this!" I cried, pointing to my
purple and swollen bare feet.

"I know babe."

"What is *wrong* with me!? I can't even stand
still for two minutes without my feet turnin' beet red
and throbbing. I can't eat tomatoes anymore cause my
friggin' tongue starts burnin' so bad I have to wait ten
minutes before I can even eat again! I do nothing but
cry all the damn time-"

"I know baby."

Joe didn't know what else to say, he'd watched me break down like this more than a few times. This was just one of those days I'd reached my limit.

"I've gotta go get checked out for food allergies or somethin'! Obviously I'm not right, and I'm tired of feelin' like complete shit all the time! I can hear fluid movin' in my ears every time I turn my head, my gums bleed when I'm in the middle of a conversation, I feel like I have the flu two and three times a week! I feel like I've got ovarian cysts constantly about to rupture. I'm just, I'm SO fuckin' over not feelin' good enough to even fuckin' go out! I can't even have a good time and get a break from everything cause all I have the energy to do is lay in bed and cry! So now you get to listen to your goddamn newlywed wife have another breakdown!"

"I know baby, I know."

We were supposed to go meet some friends for a drink downtown. I was standing there in my underwear with half my makeup done, and soaking wet hair dripping down my shoulders. I was still holding the mascara wand in one hand and sobbing into the other while I curled my knees, wishing I could just fold in on myself and disappear. I hated Joe seeing me like this.

"What has he gotten himself into." I thought.

He sat down on the bed, now looking like *he* wanted to cry, slowly untied his shoes, and put his sweatpants back on. He crawled under the covers facing me, and pulled the comforter back for me to climb in next to him.

I was so fucking tired.

A few months after our wedding, we'd moved to Mooresville North Carolina. It was time for a new start, and a company Joe had wanted to work for since he was a kid, had posted an add on Craigslist. I knew if he was offered the position, we had to try. His aunt and uncle were kind enough to let us crash with them until we found a place of our own closer to work, and it wasn't a month after we moved into our own house downtown, that my health ate pavement.

I was sitting in Dr. Caswell's office in downtown Charlotte, the best doctor I could find, a week later. I placed my purse on the floor next to me and tucked my leg underneath me as I sat, same as I always had at the therapist's offices, ready to get down to business. Tell me what's up, I can take it.

"You've really had a *lot* goin' on I see…" His eyes widened as he flipped through the thirteen page questionnaire I'd filled out prior to our visit.

291

"I mean, I guess?" I shrugged, "But I mean, not all that stuff's goin' on *all* the time, just on my worst days ya know. I just wanted to play it safe and come in and see if there's anything I can change in my diet maybe."

The sweet look he gave me over his glasses let me know alongside the possible food sensitivities, he was pickin' up on some serious denial.

We ran through test after test, muscle testing and going over blood work. He pulled is chair up behind his desk so we could discuss our next steps. I genuinely liked this guy, he was an older jovial fella with years under his belt. His laid back but passionate demeanor made me excited to find answers even though it might be a hard road ahead.

"Well," he sighed, "I really don't wanna be the bearer of bad news but, you're reacting to *all* foods. More specifically, I believe you may be reacting to all lectins…"

I didn't really catch much else of what he said, I was just biting down on a smile and nodding my head as if he was describing the seasoning on my dinner order. Internally, I was rapidly deflating.

"No no, it's not your fault!" I assured him, "So ok, well, um…"

I was supposed to go pick up dinner at the grocery store as soon as I left his office, "So. What *do* I eat? Where should we go from here?"

"Obviously you can't just live on water!" he laughed sympathetically, "I'd like you to get some further blood work done. Let's get a full thyroid panel and stool samples sent off because we need to really know everything we're up against here. At next week's appointment we'll go over your thyroid panel, so the sooner you can get that done the better, and we'll work on calming your body and getting it re-acclimated to some of these foods so you can start eating normally again. Sound good?"

I chuckled and nodded in agreement, again thankful for his jovial personality, "Yes, that would be amazing. I really appreciate it Dr. Caswell. I'm excited to finally start getting some answers."

"Absolutely. We're gonna get this figured out, don't you worry!"

I made it halfway down I-85 before I started bawling my eyes out. I made it to the Food Lion parking lot, looked at the entrance and cried some more. I cried in parking lots a LOT that entire year actually, it was pretty much my signature move. A serial parking lot sobber. And look, I myself am a people watcher, I like scopin' out the area, but for some reason, I think that if I park four lanes away all to myself, that no one will see me ugly crying and yelling into my phone. That no one will eeeever know...

Oh they know.

They absolutely know, but most people are just kind enough to let me snot into my shirt sleeves in peace, acting as if they saw nothing. The best (the fucking worst) is when you've cried so hard you get those awful red splotches on your face, but you *gotta* get in and buy toilet paper and orange juice. So ya blow your nose, put on your sunglasses, and walk inside to grab your shit, hoping you've completely fooled everyone. Lookin' like Lindsay Lohan sneakin' from the paparazzi, minus the fame and the actual presence of any kind of paparazzi.

That shit'll humble ya real quick.

Despite his positive approach, every visit with Dr. Caswell just seemed to get worse, and worse. My general blood work panel had looked great, "You could be an astronaut!" he'd laughed, but my thyroid panel, didn't look good at all.

"You have an auto immune disease," he said, "unfortunately this is something you're gonna have the rest of your life, BUT, there's a lot we can do so your body begins taking in nutrients again and getting some weight back on you."

He continued explaining what having an auto immune disease meant exactly, and that my body was attacking itself, and producing antibodies against my thyroid.

I thought about my dad sitting on the end of my bed laughing at my self-loathing dramatizations. The nights I sat awake clenching my jaw in a cold sweat and he'd assure me over and over, "It's *all* in your head Rebecca, you're doin' it to yourself."

Now here I was.

Again.

Attacking myself. Inflicting my own illness.

What the fuck is my problem…

I think it was a combination of the Iodine supplementation I was prescribed, and general anxiety about the whole situation, but my heart palpitations got worse overnight. I was having a hard time taking a full breath. I felt like there was a rubber band around my diaphragm keeping the air from running deep enough, it was sending me into nightly panic attacks just trying to breath.

Also, for the *love*, please don't do like I did and sit up at 3am Googling the worst possible outcomes of your illness. It just don't help y'all, it don't.

Joe was working two and three extra shifts some nights to help pay for the constant tests. He'd call me every fifteen minutes to make sure I was ok. One week that I was particularly struggling, he rushed home to find me crying on the couch with Gilmore Girls on (my form of Xanax) trying to breath, absolutely terrified I was about to have a stroke. He'd lay me across his lap with his hand on my chest, trying to breathe with me and calm me down.

He was just as terrified as I was. When doctors seem to know the seriousness of your illness and details of its effects, but *not so much* at all about the actual proven protocol to *treat* it? Well that leaves a *lot* of room to just freak the fuck out on your own.

At this point I'd been diagnosed with Hashimoto's, but the grocery list of symptoms seemed to me like it could go along with twenty other illnesses. I was then informed that once you have one auto immune disease, it's pretty much a given that you'll end up with seven or more, depending on how well you take care of yourself.

It feels like someone telling you that you're on a speeding train that's steadily running out of track, and they *may* have a way to slow it down? But in the meantime, they'll be coming around with the snack cart so it'll be fine! Oh yeah but no grains, gluten, corn, soy, dairy, nightshades, or sugars ok? So enjoy the complementary ice! Oh yeah but make sure it's distilled.

Some days, for those of us dealin' with mystery chronic illness, it's ok to just say, "*Fuck* this is hard."

I was lucky to have JoJo, who'd dealt with serious illness her entire life, and she coached me through a lot of what she anticipated I'd experience.

"If people ask how you're doing, but then interrupt you and change the subject, *don't* take it personally. Sickness makes people uncomfortable, most the time they don't even realize they're doing it. That's why I just started telling people I'm fine a long time ago. They really care and wanna ask, but girl most the time… they can't handle it."

And she was right.

I realized this wasn't just a reality check for me, but everyone around me. Just like death can bring out the weird in people, a drastic change in health and lifestyle can make people recoil in discomfort, they just

297

don't wanna hear it. Thanks to Jo's wise advice though, I knew it wasn't personal, I could kinda laugh when people were quick to change the subject or look away when I answered them.

Christa came to town for a much needed visit the weekend I got my stool test kit from Dr. Caswell, which consisted of three days of poop scoopin' and saliva samples. Christa's laugh alone brightens your spirit, so her timing couldn't have been more perfect. She throws her head back, erupting in hysterics, and clapping her hands together which are undoubtedly adorned in brightly colored acrylics.

It's the best.

She and Joe and I had a celebratory breakfast downtown on the third and final day of my kit. We then returned home so I could stretch cellophane across the toilet seat and crap out what pride I had left. They sat in the living room yelling like sports broadcasters, "How's the consistency? Did ya catch it all? How's it measuring?"

"Welp, uhhh, just shakin' uncontrollably from the pot of coffee I had at breakfast to *make sure* I could poop, and uuhhh now I'm just tryin' to shovel enough fresh turd into this tiny little tube with the Baskin

Robbins sample spoon they gave me so uh… Yeah! I'd have to say I've never felt more sensual and seductive."

I'm so glad she was there for that. I mean I know sometimes as friends we just share way too much information anyways, *but*, those are the moments we need someone there laughing with us in the worst way.

These things have a way of highlighting relationships in your life that are gonna make it through anything, and the ones that'll stay running so long as you act like nothing's changed and you listen to what came in their glam bag this month. Not to say these changes or realizations happen overnight, but once you hear the silence on the other end of the phone, things can never really go back to the way they were.

Maybe even worse, ya also start seeing who gets off on watching you fail, who's been quick to run to your side, not to help you celebrate the wins, but to secretly delight in your despair. *That's* not really so fun to see either, but, it does turn out to be a blessing later, I promise. Manipulation's tricky like that, you'd think people wouldn't run to you for energy when your battery's running at its lowest, but as it turns out, those kinda people run on a different kinda power all together.

The negativity that drains *us*, that wears us down and makes us sick, actually fuels and invigorates them. These people are like ghosts, not creating their own light from within to share and live happily, but instead they're constantly seeking energy to sustain themselves.

If there's not a dramatic situation, magnified and explosive emotions for them to pull energy from, to gain attention, they'll simply lie and create one. Simple as that. No matter how much light and happiness we try to throw at these people, they survive on the opposite, so joy is *not at all* what they want from us.

I was repeatedly warned by my dad when I'd sometimes driven his diesel truck as a teenager, "Now I don't wanna have to rebuild that engine, so *do not* forget and accidentally put gas in that thing!"

I think this is kinda what it's like trying to fill and satisfy a narcissist with love and compassion, it's just *never* gonna work baby. They're not built to run on that stuff. And no matter how much we may try to convince them there's a better life, they can heal, they can change... most people don't even wanna have to rebuild an engine, not to mention themselves.

CHAPTER TWENTY

"She's overachieving, chasin' her dreams
and coming down slowly, yeah its outta
control."

Moaning Lisa Smile

Wolf Alice

*I*t was time to get a second opinion. We'd
uncovered so much with Dr. Caswell, discovered
parasites, and abundant strains of Streptococcus and E.
Coli, and we knew if we were gonna continue maxing
our credit cards out further, another opinion wouldn't
hurt.

I had all my blood work faxed to another doctor
in the area, Dr. Eldridge, who had rave reviews with

stage four cancer remissions and specialized in thyroid disorders. The lady knew her stuff. She also scared the ever livin' daylights outta me.

Our first visit together lasted every bit of three hours and I don't think I ever spoke but two sentences. (Word to the wise, that's kinda a bad sign when the *patient* is the one holding all the clues. Remember that for yourself.) I was there for my second visit after she'd gotten a chance to look through all my tests so far.

"I'm not one to fool around, I like to get right down to business." She snapped.

"Yeah sure, I respect that, so what's up?" I said.

"To be blunt, these are the worst thyroid numbers I've ever seen, and my daughter was born *without* a thyroid. I mean, .001? This isn't good at all Rebecca. Not at all."

I felt my stomach getting hot and my palms sweating like I was sitting in the principal's office.

"We need to hit this *hard* and get you on a protocol today, cause from where you're sittin' right now, you're gonna be in the hospital within the next month."

She continued flipping through the results shaking her head and sighing, as if my bloodwork was personally insulting her very profession. I needed help and straight facts, *not* to be horrified by the surety of my impending death.

She handed me a twenty page laminated booklet she'd put together for me with all the results, full body detoxification protocols, and a long list of supplements to be taken immediately. The first page had a heading reading: *Top Four Causes of Death*, with a bullet point list underneath and Auto Immune circled heavily in red pen. In case I happened to miss *my* cause of death in the lineup.

"I wanted you to see this Rebecca, it's not meant to scare you, but you need to know the severity of what we're dealing with here. I mean from what I see in your blood work, well, lemme just show you."

She slammed a heavy text book on the table and flipped to a page reading, Hyperthyroidism and Grave's Disease. She skimmed through a few symptoms and again started shaking her head.

"Now, we're gonna *hope* this isn't what we're dealing with, cause if it *is*, this is gonna be a lot harder than we thought, but we need to be prepared."

"Well like, what makes it worse?" I asked shaking, "I mean what changes would need to be made in case this *is* what I've got goin' on?"

"You could very likely suffer from a stroke, serious heart damage, all kinds of things, but this is just a hypothesis right now. We still need more blood work done before we can really know."

"Ok."

"So for right now, we're treating you for hypothyroidism, we're gonna move forward with a Hashimoto's protocol because I'm not wasting anymore time. We've already wasted enough!"

"OK so, we'll treat this as hypothyroidism for now rather than hyper? But, then, what if it turns out it *is* hyper? I mean the hyper looks more like what I'm experiencing with significant weight loss and-"

"Yeah well!" She interrupted, "*He* probably threw you into hyper by prescribing you iodine! Unbelievable…" Throwing my former evidently under qualified and ignorant doctor under the bus.

I thought about my dad starting conversations with, "Rebecca, the things your mother's done to you… the things I could tell you… You wouldn't even believe."

My stomach was in knots and I was trembling thinking about the fight I had ahead of me. I was already exhausted. I'd already *been* exhausted. I looked over the list of supplements she gave me.

"Ok I understand, but, you have thyroid hormones listed on here, wouldn't that *not* be a good idea if it turns out I'm already producing *too many* thyroid hormo-"

She snapped and interrupted again, "That's not gonna make a difference! I know what I'm doing. I want you to begin these protocols today. Take this list to Lab Corp and have the results sent to me immediately, and I'll call you as soon as I have them in front of me."

I stood at the reception desk, searching through my purse for my wallet and sweating through my jacket.

"Will you be purchasing any other supplements today or would you like to wait?" the receptionist asked sweetly.

"Um I guess… the L-Glutamine power and the thyroid hormones."

"Ok great! I'll grab those for you, just one second!"

She bounced to the wall of bottles humming to herself as I ran my eyes down the list of pills and powders, trying not to cry as I calculated the numbers in my head. This was gonna be more than our rent just for a month's worth of supplements, and that didn't even include the cost for each visit or the other treatments she wanted me to do.

Ohfurrfucksake...

My sister had asked me to keep her updated, so for the last two months I was calling once a week, and I hated that it was never with good news, but I'd managed to keep it cool and act positive.

I couldn't help but start sobbing when she picked up the phone this time though. I was scared.

"Sissy this is just... not going well. I'm tryin' to stay positive but this lady says I'll be hospitalized before the month's out and the supplements alone are gonna cost more than our rent. I'm just so scared I'm not gonna be able to have babies-"

She interrupted with a heavy sigh, "Rebecca... I know you're havin' a hard time right now and all, but I just can't really handle any more of this. I have my own stress to deal with. So, from now on, if it's not inside my four walls, I really just *don't* wanna hear it."

It wasn't the first time she'd said something like that, but I was still a little stunned. But I get it, I knew her hands were full with the kids, she didn't need me being a Negative Nancy. I felt ashamed for always calling her when I was struggling, I didn't realize it was that bad.

"I understand, I'm sorry, I didn't mean to wear you out. I'll just, I'll let you know later I guess if, anything really changes -"

"You'll be fine." She snapped, and hung up the phone.

I remembered calling her in desperation the nights my heart was breaking, when Dad would walk right past me in the kitchen as if I didn't exist. As if I no longer deserved recognition at all. She'd driven home, I thought to defend me or talk some sense to him, but it had always turned out to be so she could yell at him for herself. To start up a whole new fight, and then I was left in a worse situation than before. She always came running to my side when I was at my lowest, and then left as soon as I admitted I was losing hope.

But I thought we'd outgrown all that. I thought that was all just our worst sides coming out because of the divorce.

I called my dad the next day as I pulled out of the Lab Corp parking lot, he'd also asked me to keep him updated. Just the simple fact of him answering my calls, made me feel hopeful.

"Well, I called 'n had em put your name on the prayer roll, but, *I* think you're gonna be just fine," he said, acknowledging my obvious dramatizations once again, "I'm sure it'll turn out to just be a little bug or somethin'."

A *bug*?

"Yeah I know…" I said, starting to cry but trying to act unbothered by his nonchalant attitude, "We'll get it handled, it's no biggie. I just, figured I'd keep ya updated, letcha know where we're at with everything."

I felt like I was just exhausting he and Sam both. Calling them to whine and cry like a child about my trivial problems once again. The fact that he put my name on the prayer roll gave me hope that he at least somewhat took me seriously. I mean he *had* to care a little bit if he bothered to do that!

But let's be honest, it's not really a huge feat to put someone's name on that list. I guarantee there's shrouded Mormon's circling an altar at this moment, sending prayers to someone's Duke Energy bill. At this point though, I was hanging on to threads.

I'd driven 3,000 miles after hearing my dad's voice over the phone when Janice was diagnosed. I could count on two fingers how many times he or my sister had visited me in my entire life, and it was because they needed something. After seeing my weight plummet and my health deteriorate, my mother's big concern was, "Rebecca are you *sure* you're not doing any extracurricular activities?" As in hard drugs. Which, I was beginning to realize, slowly but surely, that bath salts may have been less detrimental to my overall health than continuing to beg for validation from my immediate family.

Funny how my mom still manages to shed light like that.

I had friends and cousins and aunts that filled in, that called me before I had the guts to say I needed them. People that stepped in to help when I didn't know how to ask for it. I sat in a parking lot sobbing after work, waiting until Joe's mom and Pop's left before I went home. My muscles had gotten so weak I couldn't start our push mower, so they drove an hour and mowed our lawn for us, and I could *not* face them.

I felt so ashamed. I wasn't bleeding from my eye sockets, I didn't have terminal cancer, I wasn't 9 months pregnant! I should've been able to mow our fucking lawn.

These two sides of me fought back and forth daily. One side felt like I was just using everyone for attention, exhausting everyone and ruining their lives. All those times I'd been called too sensitive, the trouble maker, and the family hypochondriac came screaming through my head, reminding me how many times this had happened already. It was *always* me.

Both doctor's weren't happy that I was still doing massages, but I assured them I was fine. I needed to make money, and deep down, the illness was probably my own doing. I was just a rotten person who was unconsciously making herself sick to get attention. It didn't matter what my blood work said, I just needed to buck up and stop complaining.

But another side of me, the one who'd cried for so long saying, "I'm just *so* tired," knew enough was enough. That I'd been fighting for too long and my body just couldn't take anymore. It didn't matter who believed or if it made sense.

I either had to learn to believe myself, or I was gonna die.

I could feel my body shaking in a constant state of terror, and my heart thumping out of rhythm in my chest. All tests and diagnoses aside, I knew deep down my body couldn't last like that for another ten years.

I couldn't remember a time that I wasn't white knuckling the blanket at night, gritting my teeth so I could keep smiling, or faking a yawn when my eyes filled with tears. My happiness had reached such incredible heights throughout my entire life, to only stay tied to this awful weight that settled in my feet, making it harder and harder to keep putting one foot in front of the other until I physically struggled to stand.

Joe had ran into the bathroom years before in Wilmington, scooping me out of the bathtub after he'd heard me calling to him. I was trying to relax and take a hot bath after another stressful day with my family. I was sipping water from a mason jar, and realized I couldn't unclench my fingers from around the glass. My muscles started curling in on themselves and I sobbed to him, terrified, not knowing what was happening. My legs curled to my chest and my body shook as if I was in shock.

It happened again while we were living in Mooresville. I used coconut flour to make a recipe and I think the fiber was just too much for my body. I got violently ill, making it through my 9am massage the next day and racing home to get back in bed. When I tried to get up and use the bathroom a few hours later, but realized I couldn't stand, I called a friend to help me. I crawled to the living room, unlocking the front door and pulling myself onto the couch. My entire body curled into the fetal position and pulsed with pain. She sat across from me as I took sips of the Gatorade she'd

311

brought. My muscles slowly started to release and twitch as they let go and I was able to breathe again.

I couldn't keep living like this, there was no way.

Dr. Eldridge finally called with the results from my latest blood tests.

"Hey Rebecca, I've got your results sittin' infronta me," she sighed.

"That's great! Ok so what are we lookin' at?"

She went on 'n on about hemoglobins and goblins and a bunch of shit that had nothing to do with the answer. I let her finish her monologue and finally cut in,

"Ok but, so like, am I treating *hypo*, or *hyper*thyroid? Cause I'm on a diet and your supplements for hypo, so I don't wann-"

"I can tell you that when you come in for your next visit."

"No no, can't you just tell me now if I should be eating for an overactive thyroid? I mean you already explained how seriously detrimental it is for me to eat foods to activate the thyroid when it's already overactive. You said I'd be waiting to have a stroke-"

"*Again*, I can't really give that information to you over the phone."

This bitch…

"Well you're *gonna* tell me somethin' cause I'm gonna end up havin' a stroke before our next visit from the stress! So, *please* just tell me, should I be eating for hypo or hyperthyroidism? That's all!"

I could feel her eyes squinting over the phone, "…At this time, I think it best you structure your diet to be beneficial for an overactive thyroid."

"Thank you! That's *all* you had to say!

Needless to say, there was no next visit. I'd had it with the fear tactics, my adrenals were shot to hell already. I didn't need to be put under more unnecessary stress.

I found the best endocrinologist in our area specializing in Grave's Disease, and once again went through the process of faxing all my paperwork and going to get further blood testing done.

I'd maxed out one card and was working on my second, when Joe's job announced they'd be laying off eight hundred employees, and since he hadn't been working there a full year yet, we knew he'd be one of them.

My food prep alone was taking two to three hours a day, and I'd been instructed to get a minimum of ten hours of sleep a night, preferably with a two hour nap in the afternoon. My weight had dropped to 98 pounds, and this was while I was eating a grass fed beef patty, chicken sausage, steamed chard, homemade sauerkraut, and a steamed sweet potato with bone broth just for breakfast.

I stood eating spoon fulls of coconut butter in the employee room between clients, trying to keep fat on. Most days after work I didn't have time for a nap because I was busy scooping marrow from the chicken bones I'd had boiling in the crock pot. It was just... *non*stop.

Somehow though, by the grace of God, Joe and I managed to keep laughing and having a good time. I'd pouted to him on the couch, flipping through books and books on the Auto Immune Paleo Diet, "I *just* wanna keep coffee. It's my *one* vice!" Then, forty-eight hours later, we read through my detox protocols from Dr. Eldrige, and weekly coffee enemas was right at the top of the list.

He started laughing hysterically as I rolled my eyes, "That's *not* what I meant." When someone asks how I take my coffee, I assume they're asking about cream and sugar.

Not anal.

Y'all 'n it's the *worst*.

314

When ya can't actually *drink* the coffee, but you're farting Folgers. Water water everywhere and not a drop to drink. It's just cruel and I don't recommend it too highly. It'll break your lil caffeinated spirit.

Our marriage was truly put to the test. Joe'd regularly walk in the kitchen to find me filling my beautiful stainless steel enema bucket. The silicone tubing would be hung over thumbtacks above the counters like Christmas garland, real shitty Christmas garland… so as to keep the coffee from running out onto the floor.

I knew we were gonna make it when he walked up to the nozzle hanging above him, and started mimicking a caged hamster pawing and struggling to reach its water bottle.

Love and marriage.

He was always so good about making me laugh and reminding me he *still* wanted to have sex every minute of every day. I didn't realize at the time how important it is when we're losing everything we thought we were, to be reminded we're still desirable. Eeeeeven when I was at my worst and yelling about hemorrhoids and could he back away from the bathroom door cause it was about to get loud.

I never expected our first year of marriage to look like that. I always had an idea of what the perfect relationship should look like, but that image was changing fast. Fading from perfect to vulnerable and unconditional.

CHAPTER TWENTY-ONE

"I never know how to treat you. You say
I love you but it ain't true."

Hang You From The Heavens

The Dead Weather

*L*uckily when the layoffs happened, the guys got a couple months pay to cushion em until they could find other employment. We took it as an opportunity to take a long weekend to go home to my dad's and visit my sister and the kids.

Joe sat at the kitchen counter flipping through a Harley manual while I sorted out beef and chicken sausage patties to put in Ziploc bags for the trip. Then I just needed to bake some sweet potatoes and bottle a few batches of kefir before I got laundry done and showered to get on the road. I looked at the time and the to-do list in front of me, and just lost it.

I burst into tears, slamming the lid down on the cooler, and kicking it across the kitchen,

"I fucking HATE THIS! We're gonna be gone for *three days* and I have to prep and pack like we're moving into a bomb shelter! We have to fill a damn cooler with ice and groceries just so I can leave the fucking house! I'M SO TIRED!!!"

"I know baby." He let the pages fall shut in his manual, and rested his chin in his hands. "You know we don't have to go."

"Well I mean THEY'RE sure as shit not gonna fuckin' drive *out here* to see *us*! So it's fine… I'll just pack up everything and exhaust myself as always because for *some reason*, I actually *want* to make the effort to see my family, and the truth is, they've never done that for me. EVER! So if I don't make the effort, I'll never see em. It's whatever. I'll get over it."

I'm usually in the middle of apologizing for my dramatization and saying it's really no big deal while simultaneously wheezing and crying harder. I slumped down against the cabinets and tucked my knees to my chest.

Joe slid his chair back to stand up, leaned down and kissed my forehead, and quietly slid the cooler back up to the stove, and bagged the rest of the beef and chicken to be put on ice.

It was about a seven hour drive, and we got there sometime after midnight and passed out in the guest room, excited to see the kids the next day.

I woke up early, already on the brink of tears before I even got outta bed. I *always* cried at my dad's and it drove me crazy!

Joe rolled over, wiping my cheek and making a face, "I don't know what the hell is *wrong* with me!" I said. The kids peaked through the door, as I quickly wiped my eyes, "It's time for breakfast Aunt Sissy and Unca Jooooe!"

We got dressed and went outside to grab the cooler outta the car.

"Ya ain't gonna eat pancakes with us?" My dad said as I started unloading groceries.

"I know… I wish I could. I can't really have pancakes right now, but they smell delicious!"

He wrinkled his forehead and rolled his eyes, "Your loss."

"Yeah! Tell Aunt Sissy that's fine, more for us!" Samantha chimed in, egging the kids on as she fed her youngest at the kitchen table.

I laughed and looked away hiding my eyes and swallowing the lump in my throat. This was gonna be a *long* 72 hours…

I sat down at the table with my meal just as everyone started to pour syrup and slather on the butter.

Samantha gave me a look and laughed at my plate, "You're gonna eat *all* that?"

"Yep, it's actually pretty good! It just takes gettin' used to, havin' burger patties for breakfast 'n what not."

Everyone rolled their eyes, acknowledging my obvious need for attention. Joe squeezed my hand under the table and tried to get me to look at him but I couldn't, I was already trying not to cry.

The first year of me and Joe dating, my mom wanted to make dinner for all of us, and excitedly said she'd make a salad *especially* for me since I couldn't do dairy, and everything else would have loads of butter and milk. We sat down at the table and I assessed the spread,

"Hey mom, before we pray, *real quick*, where's the salad?"

She looked at me confused, and pointed to a bowl of whipped hot pink fruit salad, "Rebecca, it's right here."

"Uhh, Mom? You said you'd made a salad for me, cause you knew I couldn't have dairy. That's straight up Cool Whip."

"Oh Rebecca! You didn't tell me what *kinda* salad! Oh for heaven's sake. I guess now you're not even gonna eat any of it…"

This was an ongoing theme in our home.

I'd try and make things easy and have a separate pot on the stove of green beans or potatoes, and come downstairs to see Samantha cutting an entire stick of butter into it.

"Oh I'm sorry, was this for *you*? Oops"

Nothing gets me quite as upset as if you mess with my food.

But I digress. Continuing on with the awkward breakfast-

"Tell Aunt Sissy that's just *wrong,*" Dad whispered to the kids, shoving a handful of pancakes into his mouth and dancing in his seat mocking me, "Mm mm mmmm, she sure is missin' out!"

"Yeah Aunt Sissy, you sure are missin' out!" they mimmicked.

I wanted to stand up from the table and make a public service announcement, "OK! Can we just make it clear that I would *love* to have pancakes and hot chocolate for breakfast, but I *cannot* right now. We all know I'm not eating like this just for kicks right? Y'all *do* know that right?"

The conversation went on, condescending remarks about my job and questions about whether I was even getting any clients. We won't go into all those details but let's just say, the Himalayan sea salt on my baked sweet potato, was *significantly* less than the amount running through my veins in that moment.

I was constantly under scrutiny, but no one else was ever even questioned. Ever. I remember we were all laughing at the dinner table one night when I was twelve, and I jokingly referred to my dad as a bonehead. He did not speak for the rest of the meal, and proceeded to get up from the table and lock himself in the office for the rest of the evening.

We never spoke of the atrocity again.

And here I was, defending my right to just eat a *damn* sweet potato, so I didn't have a mouth full of canker sores for the next week.

I gave myself a time out as everyone finished their plates and retired to the living room to get on their iPads. Joe got cartoons going for the boys and I hurried to take my morning supplements before anyone could make another comment.

I was just finishing mixing my L-Glutamine powder into a glass of orange juice when my dad came in making a face,

"What's thatcha got there?" He said.

"Oh it's just some powder to help repair my gut lining."

"Yuck." He gagged, "no thank you." and grabbed a handful of peanut M&M's from the counter.

Even now, I cry because I feel like *such a fucking child* even thinking this way, but ONCE, just once, I wanted someone in my family to sincerely ask me, "So what's your next step? How you feelin?" Without adding to the end of it, "I'm sure you're just overreacting. It's nothing."

I started sobbing shortly after that and hurried up the stairs before anyone saw me.

Joe walked in and I was sitting on the bed with a roll of toilet paper, dabbing my eyes.

"I dunno what my problem is." I said shaking my head and throwing up my hands in disgust, "I mean, I can't even fuckin' make it ten minutes without crying. 'N I don't want the kids being around this, they don't need to see Aunt Sissy havin' a friggin melt down. We just got here 'n I'm a freakin' basket case, why should we even stay if I'm gonna be like this."

"I dunno babe.." He sat down next to me rubbing my back, outta answers and not knowing what to do himself. "You want me to get you some water or somethin'?"

"No, I just, lemme just get myself together. I'll be back down in a minute."

I listened to him go back down the stairs, wondering what he must be thinking to himself about me crying, *again*. I tried to slow my breathing and talk myself down. You're fine. Nothing's wrong. You're probably just dealin' with hormonal fluctuations from your new supplements. Don't ruin the weekend for everyone just cause you need to have a pity party Rebecca. You cry *every time* you're around your family. Stop it. No wonder everyone's exhausted by you. Just chill the fuck out, what is your problem?

I got up, checked my face in the bathroom, and walked back downstairs. Sam was at the kitchen table feeding her youngest mashed peas.

"What's wrong with *you*?" She said.

"I dunno sissy, I'm just… I dunno. I guess I'm just havin' a hard time adjusting to the new diet and supplements," I started to cry again, "I just, I don't wanna be around the kids like this-"

"Trust me, they don't even notice."

"Well, I mean, even so. I dunno what's wrong with me. I don't want us to turn around and leave but I can't stop cryin-"

"Well then maybe you *should* just leave." She snapped.

She scooped another spoonful of peas from the jar, and turned her back to me facing into the living room, pretending to laugh hysterically at something on the television.

We made it through the weekend, it wasn't pretty, and Joe and I both agreed maybe I needed to spend some time away from the family. At least until my health was doing better. We wanted to see the kids so bad, but I also didn't want them in the middle of my emotional breakdowns. I knew I had to worry about myself for now.

Money got tight once Joe's only income was coming from unemployment now, but my boss had been kind enough to give me a raise without the slightest hesitation.

I trusted my gut, stopped the paleo diet, and tried a program with powdered greens and fruits

325

instead. I couldn't even digest rice so I was sure my body needed a break from beef and chicken. Shortly after I started, I was finally able to begin absorbing nutrients again. My strength came back and I started seeing symptoms quiet down. I saw for myself that I *could* heal, and the anxiety and fear started to subside. Thank God!

I'd kept the space from the family since we'd returned home and I starting looking at my environment as part of my overall diet rather than just focusing on the foods I was eating. Even though I'd studied and taught the shit for years, toxic relationships and all that stuff, denial runs *deep*, especially when your psyche's been protecting you from the truth for most of your life.

I started looking at everything my body was expressing and manifesting as metaphors rather than panic inducing symptoms. My throat closing up and my eyes burning, I didn't wanna see the truth and no one would ever listen to me.

My legs feeling like lead pipes and my heart struggling to keep a steady beat, I was too tired to run away and the love I reached for, running through my veins, was toxic.

My entire body struggling to keep going for hours of deep tissue massages, running on nothing but

326

caffeine and power bars, low maintenance as possible…
I'd always found that the harder I pushed myself and
the less I asked for, the more likely I'd receive love.

Once I saw I really *could* do something about
my health, and the panic subsided, I started to allow
myself to soften again. I was open to listen.

Mother's Day came around, and for the first
time in years, I sent a bouquet of flowers, not like I
always had out of guilt or obligation, but because it
made me happy to think of her face when she saw them.
I wanted her to know how much I'd always love her.
That was such a gift to *myself*, to be able to really feel
love for her like that again. To feel peace with
everything she'd done or hadn't done. To be able to see
her as a person who's made mistakes and struggled just
as I have. The distance between us was working.

As kids, my cousin, my sister, and I, loved to
run around the woods with our walkie-talkies. We'd get
too close to one another sometimes and our handsets
would howl and screech loudly. We'd fan our arms
frantically yelling, "Back it up back it up back it up,"
until we could communicate without that deafening
squeal.

I feel like we can get that same feedback with
those closest to us. When heavy waves of anger and

shame are emitting from us, the closer we get it seems, the louder the howls. We try to yell over the noise, screaming and shouting, but still unable to clearly communicate. Those are the times we may *have* to put distance between us if we're ever gonna hear one another.

Walking away could be the most compassionate thing we do for ourselves and someone else. Whether they see it that way or not, we're finding a place where we can stop yelling at them in frustration and causing them further pain. We can finally begin to hear and see them clearly. We can finally love them as they are and stop trying to change them.

So now, I had to figure out how to do that for *me*. How to stand back far enough from who I always thought I was, until I could hear the truth of myself without the feedback.

All I kept hearing was, "Your sickness is as real as you need it to be."

For three or four mornings, every time I sat to journal, this memory kept popping up, but like every time it had for years before, I brushed it off. I'd had it most my life, since I was six or seven, and it had never been a big thing for me.

I'd been doing healing work as a career for *years*, and seen therapists since I was five years old. After Charles had been released from prison when I was in my late teens, I was able to walk up to him at Grandma Fran's funeral, and wrap my arms round him. How many people get a chance to do *that*? To really make peace with their abuser. To take their power back and see their attacker as the shell they are.

I'd honestly spent my *entire life* digging through my shit and healing. So I pushed that memory back again. Don't even fuckin' tryyyyyy to tell <u>me</u> I have to start over cause we ain't doin' it. No ma'am. Im fine! I'm just tryin to improve on my work thus far, I ain't tryin' to dig up a whole new project.

Did you ever watch one of your teachers in school, furiously erasing the entire chalk board, and they'd miss that *one fucking spot*!? They'd pass over it ten times and you'd wanna stand up and say, "Ohhh my gaaaahd, it's *right* there!"

That's what this *one* memory felt like. The one speck that my clean sweep missed. No matter how many times I'd told myself how insignificant it was, that it was nothing, I could never fully take my eyes off of it.

I'd never shared it with anyone. It had always just stayed hung in the back of my closet, like that ugly ass dress someone gives you, but you just don't have the heart to risk em finding it on the rack at Goodwill. So no matter where you move, or where you go, ya gotta take that stupid ugly dress you never wanted in the first place. Cause you're a nice gahdamnperson.

I finally decided if I was going about all this trouble to get myself better, it couldn't hurt to at least share the memory with one person, to just get it it out in the open and move on.

Joe was in the kitchen rebuilding his bike, and I walked up announcing I had something I needed to tell him.

"No no no, not like, about you 'n me!" His body relaxed, "It's just something I think maybe I need to get off my chest. I just need to say it out loud to someone."

He turned to face me, putting the socket wrench down and leaning against the wall, "I'm listenin' babe."

"I just, ok. It's not like, I mean, it's fine. I made peace with it a long time ago, it's not like a *new* memory or anything, but I think maybe just for my health's sake it'll help maybe…"

His eyes widened and his chin turned down as if to say, "Ok let's spit out…"

330

"Ok so, it's this clear memory I've had since I was six or seven, in the living room with my dad 'n like, I think Mom and Sam were upstairs before we were supposed to have dinner or something?"

I kept talking, telling him in detail what had happened. I didn't feel anything at all, but tears started streaming down my face, and Joe put his hands on my shoulders. I told him how I'd pushed my dad away and how when I'd gotten upset, my dad had showed no reaction whatsoever. As if what he'd done wasn't out of character for him at all, and *I* was the one acting out.

Joe's face continued to darken and I shook my head, "No no no it's really ok, I just, I'm almost done!" I continued, rushing to finish recounting the memory.

"So I jumped up and sat in the chair on the other side of the living room, we had this big reading chair that sat in the corner, and I just sat there *glaring* at him for like five minutes straight. I was SO angry but I didn't know what else to do. I remember he *never* even turned to look at me. He just kept watching the TV, like nothing had happened. I think I just finally stood up and walked into the kitchen."

Joe hugged me so tight and I pat his back signaling him he could let go now, it was fine. "It's *really* no big deal babe! This isn't anything new for

331

real, like, I've always had this memory 'n I'm fine it's just, ya know, healing wise, I thought maybe it might help to just share it. It's really nothing!"

But his eyes said it *wasn't* nothing. He looked like he'd just been punched in the gut.

I immediately regret telling him. I felt so disappointed and angry with myself. I'd never had to share this memory before, and *now* look what I'd done.

I could never take it back. Joe would *never* look at my father the same, ever. I hadn't thought about *that*. All I ever wanted was for Joe to idolize my dad just like I always had, to see him as the hero that I knew he was. What if Joe never even wanted to see my dad again? I hadn't thought about any of that.

I thought maybe I could just get rid of this stupid little memory, and once and for all wipe that spot off the glass. Now all I'd done was smear it to hell.

I'd carried this memory for so long, and managed fine, but as I walked out of the kitchen, still assuring him, "It's *really* ok babe, its fine, let's just move on." The tears kept coming. *I* wasn't the one crying. I was fine, so what the hell was my body's deal? Why was it reacting like that?

As if I really had something to cry about.

A little over a year passed.

CHAPTER TWENTY-TWO

"So take your hat off boy when you're talkin' to me."

Feed the Tree

Belly

*W*e moved to Raleigh for Joe to start his new job driving a truck. Luckily, seeing quickly that we *don't* like being apart, he found a permanent position in town. My health had drastically improved after regularly drinking greens and rebuilding my nutrient supply. I was finally not just quieting the symptoms by cutting out aggravating foods, but I was healing bit by bit.

The endocrinologist had prescribed anti-thyroid medication before our trip to Belize the year before, and within 48 hours I'd felt like I'd been hit by a bus. I quickly decided maybe meds were not the ticket for me. After the improvement I saw just from incorporating huge amounts of fruits and veggies back into my diet, and cutting down the fat, I was done with all the supplements and medications that were just throwing me into a tail spin.

It wasn't a quick fix, but it was *actually* working as opposed to masking what I knew the doctors really had no clue about.

It's not their fault, they're all workin' their hardest with false information. I may've dropped outta high school but I'm not stupid, and I'm sorry but common sense goes a long way when it comes to health. All the explanations I'd heard about antibodies, and my body just deciding to attack and destroy itself? It just sounded like a buncha bullshit to avoid finding the real answers.

Our bodies fight tooth and nail to fight off bacteria, kill viruses and heal themselves over and over every day. So a flip gets switched and they suddenly just decide to go to war with us? I ain't buyin' it toots.

It sounded to me like what's referred to as Triangulation. For example, when a narcissistic parent turns their children against one another. Whispering lies, acting as if they're in defense of one child, while building the case on how vindictive and conniving the other is.

"Oh Rebecca, I don't know *why* she'd just turn on you like that…"

I have a good guess.

The manipulator gets to step back and watch you fight it out, trying to get to the bottom of something that never even existed until *they* created it.

We get life sentences, diagnoses, and named illnesses imposed on us by people shrugging their shoulders. We're told it's *our* cross to bear, our burden to carry. It just is what it is. So we spend thousands of dollars trying to fix something that we don't even know the truth about. Trying to cure an illness someone else created to provide themselves entertainment or financial gain.

We can spend years and years healing, circling the truth but never stopping to *really* look at it. We've trusted what we were told for so long, why should we question it now?

I'll tell ya why. If it ain't workin', then it's time to throw it in reverse and find a different route. No matter how hard it is, life just ain't worth livin' knocking our heads against a wall.

I was having way more success with my health, just trusting myself.

I got a position at a beautiful med spa in town, and although I was doing much better, I was still crashing, going through boxes of Alka-Seltzer Cold & Flu during busy weeks. Joe and I both decided maybe it was time for me to just work for myself so my body could continue healing. I'd pushed myself for so long it was time to try a slower pace.

My mind was at war with itself every day after I'd shared the memory with Joe. "You've known this since you were what, seven!? Why make a big deal out of it *now*? People make mistakes, get over it." Then five minutes later, "Ok but why would you feel such disgust and shame in yourself for sharing something that *doesn't* matter? It matters. Are you sure that's the only time something like that happened, or is it just the only time you remember? Cause your dad seemed pretty calm and collected when you pushed him away."

Even as I write this now, I have to squint my eyes to remember the words I'm looking for, prying open a part of my mind that's been locked in darkness for years. It feels like dragging a foot behind me that doesn't wanna wake up yet, so bear with me, we're gettin' to the bottom of this.

Remember how I'd thought about doing counseling work before I went to massage school? Well I figured if I was gonna slow things down, it was time to start on a new venture, and I enrolled in a doctorate program specializing in Humanistic Science.

In all honesty, a big part of me just wanted to be able to correct people when they questioned me and say, "That's *Dr.* Rebecca…" Either way, the program turned out to be *way* more revealing and beneficial than I'd assumed. I cracked open my belief systems, able to do it now apart from any kind of spiritual practice or protocol, and simply be objective and observe myself without trying to fix anything. I felt safe enough now to just let myself unravel and disassemble the entire foundation.

It can be easy to go through self-analysis and just cyclically hash over the same life lessons over and over. The majority of the healing world does just that. (Sorry to say it.) Swimming through traumas and patterns but never truly tearing it down and rebuilding. It gives *us* a scab to forever pick, and a way to avoid moving forward for as long as we want. It also provides job security; a constant flow of emotionally addicted and fear driven clients for unethical and power driven therapists, psychics, shamans, numerologists, etc. We can work *so* hard at lookin' busy and righteously "doing the work," that we forever procrastinate *actually* evolving and opening to love.

We put off *actually* living.

I know. It stings a little, but most things that clean out our wounds do.

I'd been so sure of who I was as a child. I'd sat facing our church's congregation after my baptism at eight years old, wiggling in my seat with excitement thinking, "I cannot *wait* to show y'all how close I am to God!" I just felt like life was this gift I couldn't wait to unwrap with everyone. That I had this magic secret I couldn't wait to share.

I sat in front of the television watching *Shining Time Station*, I couldn't have been more than six. It was their Christmas episode. Everyone stood in the train station fighting and arguing over the ruined holiday, and a little girl walked up and started to sing. Everyone slowly stopped to turn and watch her, then joined in to sing and hold hands. I remember watching this scene with a fire in my chest, "That's what *I'm* gonna do!!!"

Then years later, having just moved into my downtown apartment in Wilmington, I sat journaling and wrote, "You <u>are</u> the woman you knew you were at six years old, and that scares the *shit* out of you."

It sure does.

I knew there were big things to come, a huge light for me to shine when I was just a child, but I had no idea what. I think more often than not, it's best that we don't know all the details. Lord knows, we got *enough* anxiety. Life's better spoon fed a bite at a time so we don't get too far ahead of ourselves or doubt the things we'll be capable of that we couldn't possibly imagine in our present moment.

Rather than studying more shamanic doctrine, or prophecies from the Dead Sea Scrolls, I crouched down to take the hand of my five year old self, the one who'd written the manuscript and doctrine of my own life. She explained to me the reasoning behind things as simple as the music I listen to or how profusely I sweat when someone mentions money.

I watched her standing on a stool, listening to that *Glen Mill*er cassette tape. Singing, "Pennsylvania six five oh-oh- OH," while peeling potatoes in the kitchen with her mom. Playing *Henry Mancini* records and dancing to *Roberta Flack.* Never listening to what most kids her age had on their radios. She'd rather play music that her and her mom could both sing, so they could be happy and dance together.

I held this little girl's hand and watched her memorizing every *Supertramp, Van Halen, and Grand Funk Railroad* song. Turning them on at full blast hoping her dad would come out of his office and sing along. Begging him to see how lovable she could really be, if he only saw how alike they were. The little girl, who twenty years later would still try to communicate to her father through music. Sending him letters in the mail from Tahoe, with CDs for him to listen to. That little girl who drove three thousand miles just to make sure her daddy was ok.

I watched this little girl grow older, walking around her home in headphones, using music to purge emotions she had no idea what to do with. Pain she had no idea the orientation of.

I saw how hard I'd been fighting my entire life for my family to feel love like I did. To see the magic of the world as I did. To stop the arguing and lying and self-punishing once and for all, but I just could never seem to stop the other shoe from dropping. I'd stood in the rain screaming and crying, trying to keep the storms from rolling in for so long that I never thought to seek shelter. I only fought harder.

I was exhausted.

"In all that time, from since I can remember," I thought to myself, "even at four and five years old, I *never* stopped fighting. I never gave up. Not once. Even when every day was a battle. Even when I sat in the snow at that creek making peace with death, I never stopped. It's ok to feel tired Rebecca. It's ok to finally look for answers now instead of another diagnosis. When thirty years of battles have yet to resolve what I've been fighting my entire life… What am I missing? What is it I'm a*ctually* fighting?"

In all the months and years I'd been preparing myself for the phone call that my mom was gone, there was this aching question in the center of my chest, "But what if you have to lose your Dad. Could you prepare yourself for that?"

I couldn't even bear the thought. He's all I ever had. My anchor to reality and safety. I'd still reached for his hand walking into restaurants as a teenager, holding tight to my steady protector.

There'd been a night when I was in the middle of a full on panic attack. I'd run to him in hysterics, gasping for air and dry heaving, and he'd looked at me and said, "Hey Fetti, (my nickname) how much did that first cobia weigh that you caught all by yourself? Do you remember?"

"Seventy five pounds!" I proudly answered. And the nausea was gone.

"See there?" He said, "It's *all* in your mind, you just gotta think about somethin' else."

How is it that people can be *so* right, and *so* wrong all at once? That statement taught me how powerful our minds *truly* are, but it also showed me how he may have been able to live in a world of absolute delusion all his life. Unbothered by his actions, accepting no responsibility.

How can our truths completely contradict one another's, while standing strong in their own defense? I think I've always thought that both sides of the battle field played by the same rules my entire life, assuming moral and righteous judgement translated the same to every side.

But the truth is, it doesn't.

It depends what side you're fighting for.

That straight line we wanna see clearly separating right and wrong, good and evil? The one we assume someone else will draw for us and tell us where to stand? Well, only our own hearts really know where that separation lies. And unfortunately, what is morally just and true, will often be persecuted and misunderstood by the outside world. Evils can be justified and explained away in order to keep abusive behavior acceptable

Truth is often quiet. It doesn't beg to be acknowledged, it just waits in the background. It respects our free will.

The thing is, self-responsibility isn't necessary when simply following the instructions of others, so often, very few people bother to pay attention to the soft hum of truth underneath the noise. It's too risky. It opens our world up to collapse, and ourselves to severe judgment.

We can decide to fight for self-enslaving beliefs our entire lives, with mountains of convincing evidence, punishing ourselves and justifying our hateful actions on those around us, but eventually, we have to take responsibility for what it is we fight for. For the worlds we build. For what we choose to believe.

I used to sit up in his office for hours as my dad recounted stories from runnin' the old scallop boat at sixteen years old. He'd run a crew out of Boston, having to make due with men that had criminal records twice his height, and been drinking seven and seven since before he was born. They mutinied against him after he found them smoking in the captain's helm. Pulling a flare gun on them, he told me he'd yelled,

"Y'all can try to tie me up, but one of ya's gettin burned!" Grandma had eluded to this mutiny story for years, saying he didn't like to talk about it, but I just smiled cause I already knew.

He told me *everything*.

I had sat across from him another night, recounting all of the wonderful memories I had with my cousin. Of building elaborate sets for days and filming movies and weather broadcasts. Riding our bikes through the paths between our houses and making forts in the woods. He just cried and cried as I went into detail of how great my childhood had been, and I remember being confused as to why he was crying so hard.

He's always been a crier just like I have, easily moved to tears by the slightest thing, but then there had been so many times he just shut down. He kept his back to me and acknowledged nothing but the television screen or his lottery tickets.

He'd had the locks changed on the doors to make sure mom couldn't get in after she left, and never got around to giving me a house key. He just stopped acknowledging my presence all together. I fought back as a teenager, stealing change out of his change jar, buying myself alcohol and cigarettes. Smoking bowls

346

right in front of him and pushing every button I could, but nothing would shake him awake.

I guess we both kinda got mutinied at sixteen.

He'd grabbed a hold of my knees at church one Sunday, shaking them abruptly and saying, "Look at these fleshy knees…" It was so out of context, and I remember thinking, "What's wrong with my knees?" Weeks later he took me out to lunch at Wendy's for what I thought was gonna be a daddy daughter day, but he just wanted to let me know I was getting chubby. "Rebecca, you don't wanna be the *fat* girl…" he whispered, squeezing ketchup packets onto his tray of fries.

Maybe not the *best* restaurant choice for such a discussion?

I remember looking past him, out the windows that overlooked the causeway. The smell of french-fries permeating from my tray that I now had *no* intention of eating. Especially not in front of him! I was terrified someone I knew would walk in at any minute, just in time to hear my dad telling me to, "Maybe cut down on the Moose Tracks ice cream…" I already knew I wasn't the pretty one in the family, but now I felt like I'd embarrassed *him* with my weight gain. That was even worse.

347

He crowned my sister prom queen a few weeks later, and I started on the Atkin's diet.

Once I got quiet time, leaving the spa world and starting these classes on my own, all these missing pages came flooding in. The full stories that had been cut from the highlight reels of my past. I started asking myself exactly whose truth it was that I'd been fighting to defend all these years.

It wasn't real fun to look at.

At all.

My entire life started exploding around me. Relationship by relationship started to unravel and crack. I'd spent the last years witnessing how fragile my *own* life was, so I was just too fuckin' tired to defend anyone else's. No more. I couldn't waste another breath reasoning away painful truths and trying to view them from another angle until they were finally justified.

Just like the eternal victim turnin' that Rubik's cube to get themselves a win, I'd been snatching it right back trying to spin it into something else every time. Something moral and just that made sense to me. Something that made me responsible so I could make it all better. I'd been playin' this damn game back and forth for a long... *long* time.

CHAPTER TWENTY-THREE

"So to bed little one, nod your head little one,

while I sing you a lullaby on Christmas Eve."

Lullaby For Christmas Eve

Jack Jones

I'd reopened the lines of communication with
my mom after moving to Raleigh, not a ton, but
checking in with her every couple weeks. It had become
tradition to take her out for her birthday on December
nineteenth every year. Sam and I would take her to a
seafood restaurant downtown where she could order
herself a lobster tail with loads of butter and mashed
potatoes.

That's always been something I loved about her,
her child like love for certain things. She always knew

exactly what she wanted for dinner to celebrate anything, lobster. And she'd close her eyes for the first bite and dance in her seat. It just made me happy to see her still get excited and delight in anything.

Sam wasn't able to make it this year, so I'd be making the drive and taking her out myself. I cried the entire drive. JoJo called, always knowing when I don't need to cry alone.

"Bec!" She squealed. I heard her lighter spark as she lit her cigarette. She's 4'9 and weighs *maybe* 100 pounds, but she is the toughest woman I know, and her strength has helped me stand up so many times. More than I can count JoJo.

I dreaded walking into my mom's house.

All I could think about was how the ladies from church had found her. The living room carpet now had bleach stains and ripples from them deep cleaning the vomit. The Christian station humming in the background just constantly reminded me of every time she kept asking me, "Is the bad stuff around again?" I knew she'd been fighting for a long time too.

I could smell unwashed plates in the sink and spoiling food in the fridge. It had gotten even worse since last time. The guest bathroom sink was filled with dirty socks, sweaters, wash cloths and makeup. It didn't look she was even using her washing machine anymore. Her new doggie came running up to me, Tibet. His thick coat was long overdue for a bath, but I was glad she at least wasn't alone anymore.

"Tibet." I smiled to myself.

Mom's always called herself a free spirit. Keeping collections of feathers, stones, and moss around the house. It breaks my heart that she's always known this about herself, but called *me* crazy to everyone she knows. She's incredible in so many little ways, and I wish she could see it without punishing herself.

"During my patriarchal blessing, he told me I'm a healer." She always aid, and I knew she was right.

I wanted to take her hands and say, "Mom, where did you lose your way? When did your medicine become poisonous? I've always believed in you, but where did *you* stop? When did you decide you needed to be punished? Why have you always created situations to prove to yourself that you deserve eternal damnation, to always keep company with these demons?"

It was hard not to just stand and cry in her foyer.

She grabbed her coat from the guest room, and gave her teased hair one more good spray. She'd moved all her belongings into the other bedroom after she'd come home from the hospital.

"I can't sleep in *that* room anymore," she said, pointing to her four post bed in her old lavender room, "Not after what happened in there."

"Understandable." Joe and I had felt the company she was keeping that night, and I couldn't blame her for avoiding those old stomping grounds.

She'd decided on somewhere new this year, a restaurant her friends had been talking about that she wanted to try. "Lead the way!" I told her. My GPS hadn't been working for months so I was hoping she knew the way.

"Make a right here!" She exclaimed, and I turned to see an old Hardee's that had been turned into an assumedly *not* upscale seafood restaurant.

"Are you sure you don't wanna do your usual spot?" I asked, "Remember I'm buyin', I'll take you wherever you wanna go Mom."

"Oh no, this is perfect!"

I slid into the booth across from her and looked at the mudslide dessert and cocktail flyer. For a few minutes, she felt like the mom I'd been missing for so long, but then her tone changed, and I remembered she was gone. She continued the same conversations we'd started when I was ten years old.

Recounting every bad decision she'd ever made and every wrong someone had done to her. Saying that if only she'd been smarter, if only she'd stayed with Dad, she wouldn't be ending up homeless. If only people would've tried to help her.

It's just never been enough.

I tried to lighten the conversation and discuss some lighter topics, but she just frowned and poked at her mashed potatoes and fried oysters. No lobster tail this year. I felt my angel scoot into the booth next to me and lay their head on my shoulder, wrapping their arm around me.

Our waitress brought me another hot water with lemon, and I wrapped my hands around it, thanking her from the bottom of my heart. Tony Bennett was singing Christmas carols over the speakers and everyone chatted around us about decorations and plans. "Please don't lose it, not now Rebecca," I coached myself, "Not in the middle of this restaurant under some cheap neon garland and plastic dinner trays."

I knew I couldn't last much longer, and I could feel my mom's animosity growing, knowing I'd be paying our tab soon and taking her back home. I watched her shake the ice in her plastic cup and slurp from the straw, digging for her last fried oyster with a heavy sigh.

Even when I was doing my best to make her happy, she anticipated her inevitable disappointment, robbing the good moments. She'd never even liked my name.

"I just don't like it," she'd say, "I wish it were at least spelled R-e-b-e-c-K…or maybe with an H at the end… I *just* don't like it."

She'd had a vision when she was in labor with me, an old woman came to her saying, "Her name is Rebecca." And when my mom shook her head in defiance, the woman repeated herself sternly, "Her *name*, is Rebecca."

She had no idea who the woman was, and I'd thought about it my whole life. I mean, the woman seemed pretty sure of who *I* was. Maybe it was a family member, or maybe the woman was *me*? Maybe I already knew what it was I came to do.

When I'd told my mom about Joe and I's engagement, she was so thrilled, reminding me how rare it is to find love like that, but then added, "I just… Mommy just hoped maybe you'd find a lawyer or doctor that's all."

354

It was always about money.

After our waitress brought the tab, I tried to keep my voice from shaking as I told her,

"I just don't know what else I can do for you Mom. If you wanted to go back to the hospital, I mean I'll take you tomorrow, but this is *your* fight. Every option we give you is just never good enough, so I just don't know."

"I just need you to love me." She said.

Like I haven't been doing that my entire life.

When someone doesn't know how to receive love, they conjure up ways to attract knock-offs, like pity, attention, and praise instead. They seek out things they can see and touch. Things they can physically possess. Things they trust can't be taken away from them ever again.

I left her house that night and thought of the wonderful mom I knew. The woman who wouldn't let us come downstairs Christmas morning until she'd made everything absolutely perfect. She wanted to see our faces when we walked into a paradise of twinkling lights, wrapped presents, and the sound of that old train set.

She put up that train set every year. Each time with more elaborate village scenes, ice skating rinks, and even a working waterfall. One year she'd forgotten to buy fake snow, so her and Dad stayed up all night grating bars of soap over the tiny little post offices and markets. Sam and I came down the stairs to her Jack Jones Christmas album playing and the smell of Irish Spring hanging in the air.

I think sometimes in searching through the darkness for so long, in trying to make sense of the unfathomable, we can get lost. We can become comfortable with uncomfortable feelings. Our views on what is right and what is good can become inverted, and we fall victim to our own abuse, reliving the nightmare we could never fix, believing the manipulative voices we've entertained for too long.

I knew the mistakes she'd made, and I've gone through years of anger, but all I could see now was what she'd been trying to do all along. It could never justify the injustices she re-enacted, but I see how she so twistedly tried to fix the pain in herself. Becoming the very monsters she screamed against her entire life.

My heart breaks for her, for the little girl waiting by the window for her daddy to come home every night. Begging to be loved and seen. I just want that little girl to finally feel loved, to feel peace and comfort. To know she is safe in her free spirit, and she doesn't have to wait at her window any longer. I know now, there's nothing I could ever give to ease that pain, not even my own life.

I got home from her birthday dinner that night, knowing that was likely the last time I'd ever see my mom. Joe held me in our kitchen, swaying me back and forth as I cried. I looked at the twinkling lights and garland I'd wrapped around our mantel, the brightly colored bulbs that reminded me of the woman who taught me to believe in magic. To always light candles and use the fancy dinner wear. To make a mess with fake snow and fill every birthday card with confetti, and never miss an opportunity to get lobster tail.

CHAPTER TWENTY-FOUR

"If somebody loved you and left you for dead, you gotta hold on to your time til you break through these times of trouble."

Times of Trouble

Temple of The Dog

*W*e were supposed to meet my sister and the kids at our dad's for Thanksgiving, but I'd gotten so sick again, there was no way Joe and I were gonna make it anywhere. We decided to try again for New Years, but by our second day there, I came down with the flu, hard. I was out cold, wrapped up in a blanket and passed out on Joe's lap the rest of New Years.

He drove us home the next day, and I barely made it into the kitchen before I started sobbing.

"This is ridiculous! Every time I get around my family, or I just go home, I get sick. And *no one else* ever gets sick! Just me."

"I mean, if your family makes you feel that bad babe, I mean, maybe you just shouldn't talk to em." Joe shrugged his shoulders, running out of ideas.

I'd insisted I wanted to go home, that it'd be fine. And here I was, barely able to hold my eyes open I felt so bad. Still trying to tell myself that nothing was wrong. That the memories meant nothing. That I'd created every problem in my own delusional mind.

I exploded.

"How can you SAY that to me!" I screamed, "I *just* came to terms with saying goodbye to my mom, and now you think I should just *not* talk to the only family I have left!? WELL IT'S NOT THAT EASY!"

Joe hung his head, "I know babe. I know I'm sorry, I didn't mean to-"

I slid my bags across the living room and walked away. I climbed back into bed, and didn't leave our room for the next five days. I could barely open my eyes, all I could do was lay there and cry.

Joe came home from work to bring me soup and saltine crackers. I felt so bad for yelling at him, but I think he knew why I was really yelling. He just kissed my cheek and asked me which soups I wanted him to make. I couldn't even remember the last time I'd been that sick. All I could do was lie there.

I argued with myself and pleaded with God, "What if this *is* the only option I have left, to walk away? I don't know if I can do this, but I know my body can't keep going through this day after day. Joe deserves better than this. He deserves for me to be happy and healthy. God please tell me what to do."

I felt well enough by the fourth day to call Samantha over the phone and warn her that I definitely had the flu and to take precautions for the kids, "Oh we're all good here," she said, "I dunno where ya got it from."

I called Dad, "It can't be the flu," he said, "Nobody else is sick. I'm sure you'll be fine once you get some rest."

I think Joe and I both knew that technically yes, this was may have been the flu, but my spirit was definitely bein' put in time out.

I had a lot to think about.

I didn't drown myself that night in Pennsylvania, but I felt like a part of me was still sitting on that creek with one boot in the water, fighting off hypothermia. How could I have cloves of raw garlic for breakfast, eat as clean as possible, take every vitamin and mineral under the sun, and *still* be the only one who gets sick? ...But it's hard to keep a hot air balloon off the ground when ya keep gettin' holes in your canvas, no matter how high you crank the gas. Ya can't stop playin' the victim role if ya keep attending auditions.

I couldn't accept that memory as truth, as the full reality of my past. I could accept that yes, I'd had suspicions, echoes of feelings and breadcrumbs my whole life, but it was easier to believe, "It's all in your head, you're just doing this to yourself. You just have to stop."

I prayed and cried again, to please be shown what to do, if walking away would truly bring me peace.

I dreamt that night that I was on vacation and soon realized I'd been sold into sex slavery. It wasn't much different from the nightmares I'd been having all my life. We were all taken from station to station on trucks, maybe about a dozen of us. On the last transport, we were tied up and bound around the fenced perimeter of a flatbed trailer. My hands were bound behind my back, and I was facing the dirt road behind us. I hung my head crying, once again, knowing no one would come to my rescue. My head bobbed up and down with every pothole we hit, until my eyes caught a glimpse of blue lights in the distance. They were breaking through the tree line, and the sound of sirens started to multiply. I wept uncontrollably.

It was gonna be alright.

Someone was coming.

For the first time in thirty years of those nightmares, I was being saved. I cried so hard in the dream, that I woke myself up from shaking.

"No." I thought, "I don't want this to be my answer. I can't do this."

I started getting better the next forty-eight hours, and the dreams became more frequent, and the messages very clear.

Traumatic situations portrayed over and over from a safe enough distance that I could witness them theatrically, as a bystander, able to step in and out of my childhood self. *I* was the one picked to go on special trips, I was the one that got to be the favorite, and then suddenly I wanted to go back home. In one dream I sat down in the sand, slamming my fists against the ground and screaming profanities, demanding to be taken home. I could feel myself yelling all the things I hadn't been able to as a child.

I woke up and thought about what my dad had said to me the second time he and Mom separated, "You're my favorite Rebecca. You've always been my favorite." He made sure Mom was standing there when he said it, and I felt ashamed. I was thankful Sam wasn't standing there with us. How could he just *say* that?

I laid there in bed after that dream and shook my head, letting out a heavy sigh and finally giving it up.

I made a deal myself, "Look, I am never gonna make you go home again, ever. We *never* have to go back there and we never have to try and act like nothing happened ever again."

The second I said those words to myself, my entire body took a deep breath, and let go. A calm washed over me, and I knew that was my answer. I felt peace.

I'd always known, but it's so hard to let go when you've been holding on for dear life for so long.

There'd been the same strange sob story over and over for the last ten years, and always completely out of context. "Rebecca, your mother *never* wanted to have sex!" And every time, like the times before, I'd make the same face, cringing, and repeating again that

that was really *none* of my business and could we move onto something else.

Everything connected. I realized just *how many* people had made these kind of remarks, these odd telltale statements and confessions to me my entire life.

I had friends that willingly admitted to being pathological liars and manipulators. Saying things like, "I'm not a nice person." They'd giggle with delight when I caught them in a lie or expressed my hurt feelings. I thought it was *my* responsibility to correct them, to make them see they weren't all bad.

I'd cried to a friend of thirteen years one night, "I know the worst things about you and it makes no difference to me! I just wanna be here for you, but you keep lying and hurting me just cause you're not happy!"

She looked at me like I was a complete lunatic for showing such raw emotion. Like I'd just shown her how truly weak and foolish I really was.

It was one of those silences you can't ignore.

I realized how many times, over and over, I'd begged for these friends to stop hurting my feelings while they just stared at me with a blank face.

"I mean at least I've never been like, *physically* abused though," I thought to myself, "like, *that's* awful, I don't know how anyone can overlook *that*…"

Again though, I had.

TJ had turned around and hit me in the arm one night, as hard as he could. He was upset with me that another guy had come over to a mutual friend's home to join all of us. My shoulder started to swell with a large green welt, and I remember everyone started getting angry and I just went outside, telling them it was nothing. JoJo yelled at him,

"What the FUCK man!? You NEVER hit a girl! EVER!"

He calmly replied, "Yeah well, *I* do."

I never saw that as abusive, I just, knew he threw temper tantrums a lot. I thought he was still just a little immature. All I ever saw was what I'd done wrong. That I'd egged people on, and so the retaliations were my fault.

But I see it now. Don't mistake bad character for immaturity. Some people never move past lying and biting.

It's amazing what we miss that's right in front of our face when we've been told our entire lives not to trust our own sight, our own minds, or our own memories.

I felt like I was losin' it. Suddenly all these things I'd made excuses for, for ten and twenty years started coming into focus and I realized *everything* I'd ignored.

Maybe it *hadn't* always been me to ruin everything.

I mean I *really* thought I had. Many of my closest friends made sure I knew their romantic relationships weren't working, because of *me*. Somehow everything always came back on me, but I was also willing to accept fault.

I thought if I took all the responsibility home with me at the end of the day, I *knew* it'd get dealt with and handled. It was my full time job. I'd always lived for the moments I could reprimand these people for bad behavior. Puffing my chest out, demanding they never show me or anyone else such disrespect again! Until the next time they did… and I was again astonished at their completely predictable behavior. That's what made these kind of relationships work, it was a constant toxic cycle where we both got to act out our addiction.

I've always been surrounded by wonderful people, but unfortunately I've let a lot of them down through the years, always focusing all my energy on saving the ones that hurt me the worst. Obsessed with the idea that one day they'd see the person in themselves that *I* saw. I'd been just as manipulative as so many of these people had. Maybe in a different way, but still fighting for control. I wasn't being a friend, I was being an unsolicited and unwanted therapist. I'd formed the exact same relationships around me that I'd had with my immediate family all my life.

I called someone I knew would be blunt and lemme know if I was just overreacting, Vern.

"But I just can't believe she could just *lie* like that. For no reason! Just cause she's unhappy and wants attention." I confided.

"BeBe," Vern said sweetly, "she's *always* been like that."

"*Really*?"

Yes really. She had.

They all had.

I never wanted to acknowledge I couldn't fix anyone, cause that meant I couldn't lie to myself about the memories anymore. I couldn't keep telling myself I was working toward a noble cause, that I could fix the past by reprimanding the future.

I realized in each and every one of these situations, the second I defended myself, I was the problem. The second I tried to get to the bottom of something, I was the one ruining everything.

Joe had shook his head so many times, hearing either my mother or sister screaming through the phone as I held it away from my face, and more often than not, they'd be screaming, "DON'T YELL AT ME!" Always about something I'd never done, but in fact *they had*, constantly. A few nights I'd woken up after those calls with swollen tonsils, and he made me promise to just hang up the next time.

I felt like I was untangling myself from a spider's web.

I poured my heart out to those friends that never left, that always stuck by me in the back ground, some for almost thirty years. And in our early thirties, let's face it, *most of us* start uncovering all kinds of family secrets, so this was right on time for a lot of long talks.

I wasn't ready to tell Joe about some of the repeating dreams I'd had, some of the memories my body was beginning to share, but again, his spirit already knew mine. I didn't *have* to say anything. He also experienced sexual violence as a child, and so he was able to hold me without judgment. I didn't feel heavy shame letting it go in front of him. His eyes said he knew exactly what I wanted to say, and I could just cry and let him hold me.

I was born with hip dysplasia, so I'd always kinda babied my hips, but I decided to see what happened if I really stuck with the pain this time. I reached the threshold I'd usually stopped at, breathed deeply, and let myself let it go. I screamed and cried as if I was going into labor, until my left leg shook and rattled until the pain subsided. There was a loud pop in my psoas muscle and I thought of how my body had gone into the fetal position those times, my muscles curling in on themselves, folding in half as if I was being attacked.

I paid attention to the intense ache that had been building in my left ovary. Clenched like a tight fist, sometimes causing me serious pain during ovulation. Never opening up to receive, never ever again. I'd been checked out so many times at the clinic, but was always told, "Everything looks great! How many sexual partners have you had?"

"Three."

"This year?"

"No ma'am, three, all together."

Slapping my knees shut as the paper underneath me crinkled,

"Oh honey, you're good to go!"

No matter how many people told me I was fine, including myself, I think I was always begging for someone to say I really wasn't.

To give me permission to admit I was hiding something. So I sought out people who pointed out every fault, every insecurity, and every doubt. I begged for other people to cut me open and look at the very things I didn't want to see for myself.

That's a dangerous thing to go searching for from wounded sabotaging souls, because what *they* find is the reflections of themselves they've always hated, projections of their own demons, and they're more than happy to hand over the ownership. We may finally turn to face the monsters in ourselves, and find out later that they weren't even ours to face.

No wonder my adrenals were shot.

I just wanted to be done with all of it. All the excuses, all of the reasoning away, all the blame that had come back on me every time. For thirty years, I'd been met with these remarks every time I expressed my feelings, or asked for honest answers. Sharp come backs and insidious statements always made to plant more seeds of shame and doubt until eventually I'd give up and realize again, it was just me. I was the one causing the problem. The one who was lost.

"What is it now Rebecca…"

"You're just too sensitive."

"That's not what I said."

"I never said that!"

"I don't remember that ever happening."

"Why are you being so dramatic?"

"I was kidding…"

"Your body's attacking itself."

"Oh it's just *all* about you isn't it?"

"One day you'll understand…"

"Well, you're not so perfect yourself!"

"I'm afraid for you."

"Well, if you'd bother to read the scriptures…"

"Yeah well, if that's what makes you happy."

"Believe what you want…"

"What about <u>ME</u> Rebecca!?"

"You're just like your mother. "

"You're just like your father."

"You're crazy just like all the other women in your family."

"If that's what you wanna tell yourself…"

"I don't have to take this from you!"

"Wouldn't *you* like to know."

"Obviously you have more healing to do."

"Are you sure you're not thinking about *my* sexual abuse memory?"

"You won't last three months without us."

Watch me.

CHAPTER TWENTY-FIVE

"This love will open our world. From the dark side we can see the glow of something bright."

Pig

Dave Matthews Band

I knew it was time to officially remove my name from the Mormon church. I researched the exact verbiage to use in my request letter, clarifying that the only further contact, should be to notify me of my name's removal.

Now I *may* have shot myself in the foot with my own sass, but I had to reward myself by signing the painfully professional and redundant letter with,

Later Suckaaaaaaas!

-Dr. Rebecca Garifo

It just gave me the warm and fuzzies, imagining some old white haired pedophile with his temple recommend tucked in his wallet next to his viagra pill, gasping at my unholiness.

It's the little things.

About a week later, I received a letter in the mail stamped, *The Church of Jesus Christ of Latter-Day Saints*. It was addressed to my maiden name, my father's name.

Excuse me but, PER my last email, that is <u>NOT</u> my name.

I opened the letter, already fuming, and saw myself referred to over and over as, "Sister (maiden name.)"

In the eyes of the church, because Joe wasn't a priesthood holder, and he and I had *not* been sealed in the temple, I was still bound to my father for all time and eternity.

You see, we aren't allowed into the highest floors of the Celestial Kingdom, unless by way of a sealed marriage with a priesthood holder. Only *then* may we receive our golden ticket to the Wonka factory at the time of our earthly departure.

"In order to obtain the highest degree in the celestial kingdom, a man and a woman must enter into the new and everlasting covenant of marriage." – Doctrine & Covenants 131:2-3

"What the fuck…" Joe said, having underestimated what it was gonna take for me to actually leave the church for good. As had I.

At the end of the letter, they informed me that my request had been denied, and that the local church bishop, whom I'd never met, would be contacting me to discuss the matter.

Abso-fuckin-lutely NOT.

I couldn't sleep that night until I found a way out. I found a lawyer across the country, who had struggled himself to have his name removed from the church. He now offers his services pro-bono for members whose requests are being ignored or denied.

Magically, the very office that had mailed me that letter, informing me it was the Bishop and *not them* who took care of such matters, removed my name promptly after one letter from the lawyer.

Imagine that.

"Husbands, love and treasure your wives, they are your most precious possessions…" - Gordon B. Hinkley, former prophet of the Church of Jesus Christ of Latter-Day Saints.

The devil's in the details.

Love that's poured on like cement. It may take a little time to solidify, but make no mistake, it's meant to keep you right where you are.

It's also never too late to ask if anyone has a sledgehammer you can borrow.

I braced myself, waiting to catch wind of my dad finding out about my name's removal from the church, breaking my eternal celestial ties with the family. Surely then, he'd know what was coming.

But there was nothing. Not a peep.

I still respected him enough that I knew I couldn't just leave. I had to tell him. I couldn't say it out loud, so I just replied to his last text message from the week before.

I told him that I knew the abuse didn't stop after Charles went into prison. That I loved him and I always would, but I knew, and I wouldn't be keeping contact anymore.

Again, there was nothing.

Just silence.

Some days I still wait for him to answer me. To say something, anything. To act like nothing ever happened, like he always had. To shame me for once again causing him unnecessary stress and trouble. To tell me again that it's all in my mind, that I'm delusional and must be hearing lies from my mother again.

But there's nothing. Just silence.

Just peace.

Some days Joe knows, when he comes home and puts his arms around me and I start to cry. He knows I've realized another month has passed, my dad still hasn't replied, and I have to accept all over again that it's real. That I'm not crazy. That every nightmare and suspicion that's haunted me for thirty years, might actually be true.

I remember during my parent's divorce, family members rushed to move a small twin bed into my dad's bedroom. He said it was for legal purposes. He just *knew* my mom was gonna say he'd been molesting me in court. He just knew it.

I was so confused. I had my *own* room, what difference was a separate bed in *his* gonna make? He was absolutely furious, running around like a mad man. I assured him, she wouldn't say that. She'd never even *hinted* at that. And if you've read this far, you know as well as I do, my mother never had a problem throwing him under the bus. "If she was gonna say something," I assured him, "She would've already said it." And just like I told him, nothing of the sort was ever even slightly suggested.

He never mentioned it again.

Joe and I made another trip to the mountains for my thirtieth birthday, shortly after I finished my Master's. We sat outside our small cabin playing Go Fish. I hadn't played since elementary school, and forgot exactly how the rules worked. Joe jokingly pointed his finger at me,

"Heeey you're cheating!"

"How? I'm sorry! I didn't know!"

"Don't you lie to me girl!" he laughed.

I started sobbing, "I promise I wasn't trying to cheat! I'm not lying! I honestly didn't know!"

I lost it.

Every nightmare that I'd had, telling me I was getting what I'd asked for when I was abused, came flooding in like a tidal wave.

Something in me *exploded*. Triggered by a game of Go Fish.

Trauma likes to show up like that, in moments we can easily see we're having an unnatural reaction.

I fought it tooth and nail. I'd been running to my dad even harder these last years, fighting against myself. Visiting once a month and begging him to turn off the television and talk to me. He'd gotten so excited when I got my doctorate, he sent money in the mail and I cried and he told me he wanted to celebrate and take me out to dinner.

We planned it for two weeks. I drove the three hours home, sick again, and cleared my schedule of massages, making sure everyone knew I couldn't work that night because my dad was taking me to dinner.

I downed medicine and kept calling him all day, making sure he remembered to get out of work in time for our date, but he never answered. Finally he called the house phone at six that evening to talk to Janice. Evidently he'd gotten stressed at work, and left around lunch to go buy himself a new three thousand dollar lawn mower.

I sat and cried.

Thirty years old with a Ph.D., and here I sat. *Again*.

I didn't wanna cause a scene, so when he walked in the door I said, "That's ok about dinner Dad, I'm sick anyways. I probably shouldn't be out in public."

He just chuckled nervously and acted like he didn't hear me, returning the conversation to the deal he got on the mower.

Maybe this is why people who've thrived on our energy and pulled our strings for so long suddenly drop us when we become seriously ill. Not only is their supply about to run out, but they're terrified to face *anything*.

They know that now we'll be on the path to heal ourselves, we'll begin searching for truth, for answers, digging through the trash and uncovering secrets. We'll no longer be giving up our light for them to consume. Maybe they have to disappear because they don't wanna be anywhere near us when the breadcrumbs inevitably lead us back to them. They're cowards.

When we start removing different medications, chemicals, vices, toxins, people, and patterns, and we see our health begin to improve, there's no denying we're onto something. There's nowhere for the secrets to hide anymore, not when there's physical proof. And so far the *only* time I've been sick ever since I made peace with the truth, was when I had to break my promise to myself, and return home for a friend's wedding. (Well worth it though boo!)

I've drank pots of coffee, whiskey and wine, and even ate a donut after almost ten years. Missed flights and slept overnight in the airport, stayed up til 3am writing and forgotten to eat for hours, and *still*, my body is doing better than it has in years. The emotions rise up, and I let the tears come out, but then it's gone. I don't have crying spells hitting me constantly or heavy clouds of depression rolling in.

Alka-Seltzer sales have surely plummeted, and for that I do apologize.

"For every win, someone must fail." - Whitney Houston

That last trip home, I'd looked again at every CD I'd sent in the mail, every movie Joe and I had bought them for Christmas, stuffed away in the guest room closet. Still in their plastic wrap, never even touched.

My dad never mentioned the letters I'd written, or the songs I'd begged him to listen to. Terrified to hear what it was I might be trying to say.

He had always reacted the same. Silence.

I've spent the majority of my life fighting these monsters. Digging my heels into the dirt begging them to release their grip on suffering. Screaming to the frightened child sitting in the dark corner of their soul, "I CAN HEAR YOU! I SEE YOU! JUST GRAB MY HAND!" But their backs stay turned. Every once in a while I've caught a small whisper, a crack in the wall, a gasp as the wounded child senses my presence like a ghost in their dark cell, but never beyond that. It's too far outside their reality that another soul could exist in such an abyss.

Even light becomes painful after being in the dark for that long.

No matter how hard I try, I can't seem to hang onto the anger for too long, my heart won't allow it.

Frankly I'm just too damn tired to stay angry anymore. It's done nothing for thirty years but keep me sick and on the verge of a psychological collapse eight days a week.

Love has to continue pumping through us one way or another, to survive no matter what it takes. Even if it means forgiving the unforgivable, our hearts will demand it to save our lives. It's when we decide to hold onto anger and resentment that our hearts dry up slowly and stop their beating year after year, until love only echoes to us from the furthest corners, locked away in that dark cell. That's when we become shells of who were were, feeding off of everyone around us just to survive.

I hold onto the good memories. Dad driving me home from my wisdom teeth surgery, drugged to hell with a blood soaked bib around my neck. I'd leaned forward to take a sip from my smoothie, and poured blood all down my chin. Now I looked like a Jamba Juice zombie riding in the passenger seat. It was a two hour ride home, and he let me play *The Wanton Song* on repeat the entire time so I could head bang and scare the people passing us. We were laughing hysterically as they sped ahead, wondering what the hell was wrong with me, and I yelled out, "YA ATH-HOLTH! YA FRIGGIN ATH-HOLTH!"

I think about the days we stood on the tower of the boat, going full speed ahead. Slamming down from each wave as the fishing rods cracked against their holders and the sun sparkled off the water. I'd shut my eyes, breathing in the salt air and think, "My dad is the greatest man alive."

I'll never let go of that. I hope someday, whether in this life or the next, his soul can heal, but it's not my job to make sure of that.

I hope every person that I've fought with for years, that I've tried to shake the love out of and reprimand the empathy into, will heal. Will learn to love themselves somehow.

I know now that my dragging them kicking and screaming, was never gonna bring them closer to that.

I'm standing back far enough now, that I can let them go to live as they wish, no longer judging and trying to control their role in this life. I can finally set them free.

I think we all deserve that.

We Made It Baby.

"Imagine entering a burning building after hearing cries for help, not only to find the person has no intention of getting out, but is now begging you not to leave them. This is no longer a rescue, but a suicide. It's ok to know the difference and save your life."

Channeled in 2018

*O*ur bodies will always tell the story. I've been shamed for starving myself, and for suffering from anorexia for years. In reality I was constantly eating entire jars of almond butter in forty eight hour periods trying to keep muscle on. My body was only screaming that it had nothing left to give. I'm constantly learning and understanding more about my health, but amidst

387

one of the hardest years of my life, it continues to flourish.

I cried so many happy tears, sitting under the moon in Belize with Joe, only a few months after telling my family that I knew the truth. I realized that not only had this been one of the hardest years of my life, but one of the best. That I'd finally done the very thing I was most terrified to do, and I was free. I never had to untangle a malicious story, or lock myself away to cry again. I never again had to agree that I was broken, that I was a monster, or that my sensitivity ruins the lives of everyone I love.

This book's been written over and over. Revised and edited for thirty-one years. I started to write it at age fifteen, wanting to help other Mormon kids who had families going through divorce. I didn't know then that there'd be far more for me to write about.

My dreams are a boiling pot of transcripts I've ripped out and stuffed under my mattress time after time. The reality of situations written in black ink, just the facts.

I see my mother walking into the ocean, deeper and deeper until I can no longer see her head above water. I hold my breath, "Come back up!" I pray to her silently, "come on mom, that's enough." No one else is watching her, no one else sees, but they scream and panic when I tell them she's gone under. They go into hysterics, begging for attention, for everyone to see *their* distress. I can't get them to think calmly and listen to me, they're swimming miles away from where she went under, almost drowning themselves.

Most of the statements in my dreams actually happened, my mind places me in a different seat so I can hear them again, witnessing the conversation one more time to see if I actually hear it correctly this time.

When I reach another level of peace, more pieces come together, and my jaw drops as I realize the reality of what I'd known my entire life. Suspicions and discomforts I had as young as five years old. I shake and tremble when I put the pieces together out loud, cry and let out a long sigh, but then it subsides. It's finally coming out.

I'm finally laying down the heavy burden that was never mine to carry. I see more of the woman I always knew I was that's been hidden underneath the weight of someone else's actions all along.

Shame's a tough shit to wipe from your shoe. Once we consciously start to release ourselves from it, our subconscious foams at the mouth in protest, pulling out a lifetime's worth of evidence to prove we are *not* worthy of love. I think this is where many of us can get stuck fighting the wrong side, begging for release and then recreating scenarios to again prove we *deserve* eternal punishment, that we are in fact the very monsters the darkest corners of our souls echo us to be.

We've got to believe in the goodness we hold.

The anger still arises and begs to be expressed, but not toward anyone in particular. Not anymore. There's no debt to be paid or vengeance to be made. I'm already free, as are those I experienced pain at the hands of. My journals may have to go through some serious ripping and tearing. I've broken pens, I've thrown plates, I scream like a banshee til the shaking's gone, but the need to wipe the shame and the hurt off on someone else?

That no longer feels necessary like it used to.

My heart understands why I've always needed those toxic relationships. Giving me constant opportunities to scream and slam my fists.

My heart knows now, to retaliate will only fuel the fire, it won't actually get rid of anything but my health and sanity. I'm learning to release my grip and allow myself to breathe again.

It's not that letting go isn't terrifying, but we regain our strength, our voice, and our power when we no longer have to white knuckle the oars. We realize we can't spend the rest of our lives trying to paddle a leaky boat, trying to "positive thoughts" our way out of a sinking stern. We can either go down with the ship, or swim until we see land. There's no telling what we'll find, but it's better than certain death. We have to try. And so we let go and start to swim.

We all have our truth. What we know to be real, justified and righteous. For some of us, our truth will mature and change over time. We will find what is truly ours, what beliefs belong to our own heart and not someone else's imposing testaments. We uncover underlying prejudices and judgements that may have caused us to lash out and point fingers at others, causing pain and separation that we now have to own up to. It's uncomfortable, it's vulnerable, and it takes time to let go of the guilt and shame, but it's *got* to be done.

It's also absolutely positively necessary, that we don't honor other's protesting and screams to the point that we let evil run over us, back up and do it again. They have chosen to see life that way, so yes, it *is* true for them, but we don't owe our own lives, to give energy to someone's destructive delusions. To forever pay the debts they've compiled. I'm here to tell ya, as many of us have unfortunately seen firsthand, pure evil believes it is absolutely right and justified and standing in *its* truth. It's COMPLETELY ok for us to say, "I hear you speakin' your truth…'n that shit is FUCKED UP."

We can become manipulated to the point that we apologize to those abusing us. We accept shame in our supposed harsh judgement, rather than honoring our divine discernment. We're told it's righteous and good and enlightened to let *nothing* bother us. To simply rise above it. To stay silent and object nothing so no one gets hurt.

No one but ourselves.

We can try so hard to accept everyone and everything and be nice, and not offend anyone, that our common sense and intuitive warnings get thrown out the window. At the end of the day, you can see the wounded child in someone, and *still* know they're quite capable of committing mass genocide. We can see where someone is in need of healing, and say, "It ain't me babe. It ain't me."

That's the hard truth of it.

In speaking our truth, we will royally piss off many hiding from it. That's part of the gig, but we're here to do it. We are just in-tune enough to see the cracks where the light can get in, whether they appear in named villains or the praised spiritual leaders of our time. Our spirit detects the need for unveiling, the need for light to be shown.

We may never be able to change others, in fact I'm pretty sure we can't, but we *can* change ourselves. The world may follow suit, or it may not, but we must begin with ourselves. That's how lasting change happens. That's how generations heal for good. That's how the abuse, the pain, the judgement, the separations, the wounding, will finally heal. We may have to learn to be ok with being named the villain, in order to be the heroes for future generations.

So here it is baby-

As Empaths, who struggle to not take *everything* to heart and people please our lives away, it's important to learn that we *will* be named the monster *many times*, and the villain of many people's story. But we can learn that bein' called a bitch, ain't always a bad thing. A lot of people use the word Bitch, when they actually mean Truth Teller, so that's ok. Us Bitches'll overlook it. We know we're makin' those that have used us nervous when we stand up. We see their knees knockin'. We've suffered the same abuse that caused them to be paralyzed in that toxic state, the only difference is, we chose to take responsibility for ourselves. We chose not to retaliate, but to heal.

We happen to be *just* sensitive enough to see every crack, every injustice, every wound, so we can end the cycle. So we can stop the patterns once and for all. So we can do what they weren't strong enough to.

And they call us too sensitive like it's a bad thing.

To be continued...

Made in the USA
Middletown, DE
22 March 2019